Barred from School

OTHER BOOKS BY THOMAS J. COTTLE

Time's Children: Impressions of Youth

The Abandoners: Portraits of Loss, Separation and Neglect

The Prospect of Youth: Contexts for Sociological Inquiry

The Voices of School: Educational Issues Through Personal Accounts

Out of Discontent: Visions of the Contemporary University (*With Craig R. Eisendrath and Laurence Fink*)

Black Children, White Dreams

The Present of Things Future: Explorations of Time in Human Experience (*With Stephen L. Klineberg*)

A Family Album: Portraits of Intimacy and Kinship

Perceiving Time: An Investigation with Men and Women

Busing

Barred from School

2 million children!

Thomas J. Cottle

The New Republic Book Company, Inc.

Washington, D.C.

Published in the United States of America in 1976
by The New Republic Book Company, Inc.
1220 Nineteenth St., N.W.
Washington, D.C. 20036

Library of Congress Cataloging in Publication Data
Cottle, Thomas J
  Barred from school, 2 million children!
  Bibliography: p.
  Includes index.
    1. Handicapped children—Education—United States.
2. Minorities—Education—United States. I. Title.
LC4031.C67   371.9'6   76-20607
ISBN 0-915220-12-1

Printed in the United States of America

*For all those people
who work in behalf of children*

Acknowledgments

This book was made possible because of the work and generosity of a great many people. I wish to thank first my colleagues at the Children's Defense Fund of the Washington Research Project, and especially the Fund's director, Marian Wright Edelman. Thank you, too, to Mr. Leslie Dunbar and the Field Foundation, and the men and women of the John Simon Guggenheim Foundation.

Special thanks go as well to Marylee Allen, Melanie Barron, Rochelle Beck, Cindy Brown, Warren Button, Audrey Colom, John Crowder, Diane Divoky, Kathleen Dyrek, Colin Greer, Paul Houts, Judith Kates, William Kates, Florence Levinsohn, Vivian Lindermayer, Cynthia Merman, Justine Wise Pollier, Charlene Sanders, Judah L. Schwartz, Alice Smith, Paul Smith, Timothy Spofford, Laurie Turner, Daniel Yohalem, and Jerrold Zacharias.

More special thank you's to Sara Lawrence Lightfoot, Orlando B. Lightfoot, Sally Makacynas, who worked indefatigably on the manuscript, Martin Peretz, Joan Tapper, and as always, my revered partner, Kay M. Cottle.

A final thank you goes to the boys and girls, men and women, whose voices are heard in this book. I am forever grateful to them for sharing their experiences with me and for granting permission for the publication of their words.

Contents

Introduction

"**E**verybody you talk to," a farmhand in rural Illinois told me once, "knows that schools aren't what they should be, aren't what the teachers of this nation meant for them to be either. You don't need to have a couple of kids in school to know that. But what this country doesn't seem to know is that the schools are bad for all the poor people, not just the black people, mind you, but all the people. That's the fact people ought to be remembering. When you got a lot of money you got a choice about what school you want your kid to go to. But when you're a little short, like they say, or when you've learned to do without all your life, like lots of folks around here, then you got to take what they give you. Now mind you, I'm no expert on schools, but from what I see, poor kids are either dying in their schools, not going anywhere, you know what I mean, or else they aren't in schools which means they're dying a different sort of death. Either way, the society's got them pinned against the trees, 'cause nobody's learning anything. Least that's what it looks like to me, you understand."

As the man spoke, he smiled as though he wanted to anticipate my response, in case I thought his words sounded foolish. He didn't want to appear embarrassed. But there was an earnestness about his report, and, perhaps, behind it, the last days of hoping that the "situation in the country," as he called it, might change. Still, everytime he fetched a new idea, the fear that in the end he was not an expert caused him to pull back, to soften his urgency, and smile his smile of anticipation.

It is four years since I spoke with him on the small farm north of Carbondale, but his face is very vivid in my mind as is my recollection of the land in that region of America and the weather of that day. He still works the same farm, and, I suspect, continues to have the same feelings about schooling and the poor. I remember his commitment to work, and to endure, but the feeling of hopelessness was never far behind his commitment. It was not the absurdity of schools or the way poor children were learning, or not learning, that touched him. It was the hopelessness, the vision of generations repeating the mistakes and misfortunes of their forebears. The details of an individual school, or a country's educational policies interested him, but not as keenly as the historical evolution of schooling and, even more, the fate of the millions of children he could only imagine attending schools across the country, and those millions kept from attending school as well.

He cares about the process, the system of education, I thought when I left him that one afternoon. He believes in the simple acts of going to school, reading books, learning about the events that, in some miraculous fashion, have brought men and women to where they now play out their respective evolutions. He cares about science as much as the development of physical strength and courage. For him, the years of learning are essential, redemptive, gorgeous. But he suffers, too, because he knows that men and women, even those of colossal intelligence, need to go to school to hear what others have to tell, and to take into themselves the public and private disciplines that schools can teach. He knows that children growing up in poverty may never complete more than a year or two of school, a bad school at that. He knows, too, for we discussed it, that even those poor children who wish to stay in school may not be allowed to complete the few years coming to them. Many are unwanted—in the country, in their town, in their school. They are tolerated, allowed to pass—in some places it is called social promotion—no matter how well they are learning, but then they are thrown back onto themselves for no one values them or their skills; they never have, they probably never will.

According to the law a child has the right to go to school. It is as simple as that. A child also ought to have the right to be fed, clothed, housed, and accorded adequate medical attention and care. These rights are not completely unrelated to each other. Many children, as we know, do not finish grammar school because they become too sick to attend their classes. They drop out, then drop away for good. Others die from illnesses that could be cured on one visit to a doctor, with a bit of medication, with a minor operation. They die because there is no medical check on them, no early diagnosis; disease festers. Strong at first, the children fight it as long as they can, unable to figure out why they cannot breathe as easily as they did last year, or run as fast, or stay awake as long as before, or sleep as well at night.

Often children fail to finish school because of devices, rules, and procedures that, while instituted in the name of learning, in fact represent political devices to further the outright strangulation of them and their families. Two of these devices involve intelligence testing and the use of educational tracking systems. Fundamentally, the problem is one of classifying students on the basis of their intellectual level, competencies, psychological states.

Children stay away from school, too, because the culture in which they grow has never been fully acknowledged by those who oversee their education. So the children are punished, suspended, deprived of the right to attend school. In this way, their biological and sociological origins are derogated and their natural development threatened. Does a school, after all, have the right to keep out a young woman of fourteen merely because she is pregnant? Is there some preordained mutual exclusiveness between pregnancy and learning? Some schools have worked out rather humane means of dealing with this condition, but most of the schools attended by poor children, children for whom pregnancy at fourteen is simultaneously not unnatural and yet perplexing, do not always honor the child's rights. Often they allow their poisonous principles to flow into the blood stream of that pregnant girl. Not symbolically, their unwarranted actions damage the seed growing inside of her as well.

Children are also out of school because they cannot pay for the bus ride to take them there or for books or clothing. Or maybe they are eneuretics, nocturnal bed-wetters, and the school demands they remain at home. Perhaps a boy has a physical illness like epilepsy or spinal bifida, and the school refuses to accept him. Perhaps the child has only recently learned English, and no one in the school will teach him to speak and read and write it well enough to pass his courses. Or perhaps the child's mother tongue is English, but her dialect offends school officials, who then refuse to allow the child to enter school. A child may be deaf, blind, or crippled, or a stammerer and be refused admission to school. And a child may be a member of some minority group, a black, Chicano or Chicana, Japanese, Haitian, Italian, and be refused admission to school.

Defining exclusion as being out of school at least forty-five days, or one-quarter of the school year, the United States Bureau of the Census reported that in 1970 2 million children were out of school. This figure amounts to between 4 percent and 8 percent of the schoolchildren in every state. More than 1 million of these children were between the ages of seven and fifteen, over 800,000 were sixteen or seventeen years old. According to the Bureau's report ten states listed more than 6 percent of their school-age children as out of school. The five worst offenders were Mississippi, with 7.8 percent out of school; Kentucky, with 7.6 percent; West Virginia with 7.2 percent; South Carolina with 7.1 percent; and Georgia with 6.9 percent out of school.

The statistics become even more striking when one examines particular age groups and minority groups. Consider the following: In twenty-five states more than 10 percent of children aged sixteen and seventeen were out of school. In Michigan, where only 3.3 percent of school-age children were not enrolled, over 14 percent of black children, aged sixteen and seventeen, and 8 percent of white children, were out of school. In the sixteen- and seventeen-year-old age group, the South is the worst offender, reporting over 14 percent of the children out of school. If one believes that the finest educational systems exist in the North, then one may be surprised to learn that 8.4 percent of sixteen- and seventeen-year-old children were not enrolled in this one region.

For the most part, nonenrollment occurs essentially at identical rates in rural and urban areas. The few minor exceptions are in the South, where 13 percent of the urban sixteen- and seventeen-year-olds are out of school, but 17 percent of rural sixteen- and seventeen-year-olds are not enrolled. This southern pattern holds for children aged seven through fifteen; of the urban children, 3.4 percent are not enrolled as compared to 5.2 percent of the rural children. In the West, 7.9 percent of sixteen- and seventeen-year-old children are out of school; 9.3 percent of rural children of the same age are not enrolled.

The most telling statistics of exclusion, however, involve race and social class. In every region and in all age groups, nonwhite children are out of school at a greater rate that white children. While the southern states, again, revealed the highest percentage of nonenrollment, the highest percentage of disparities between white and nonwhite children were found in the northeastern and north-central states. As examples, 8.1 percent of white sixteen- and seventeen-year-olds from north-central states were out of school, while 13.5 percent of black students of this age and region were not enrolled. The nonenrollment percentage of poor children follows the same pattern as nonwhite children regardless of their age or the region of the country in which they live: The poorer the family, the greater the likelihood of the child being out of school. Almost 7 percent of the children whose parents earned under $4,000 a year were out of school as compared to 2.9 percent nonenrollment among children with parents earning more than $10,000. And of those families who earned less than $4,000 and whose parents received less than eight years of formal education, 9.5 percent of the children were out of school.

Another way to examine this same pattern is to consult nonenrollment figures of various occupations of fathers. As one might expect, nonenrollment is highest among the children of farm laborers and unemployed men. The figures are 7.0 percent and 6.0 percent respectively.

As if these statistics were not sufficiently upsetting, the Children's Defense Fund report, *Children Out of School in America*, reveals that the Census Bureau's data underestimate the nonenrollment figures. In late July of 1973 and early March 1974, the Children's Defense Fund surveyed more than 3500 homes in thirty carefully selected areas of nine states. These included Alabama, Colorado, Georgia, Iowa, Kentucky, Maine, Massachusetts, Mississippi, and South Carolina, as well as the District of Columbia. The Fund's findings indicate that 5.4 percent of children six to seventeen years old were out of school for at least forty-five days—the Census Bureau had reported 2.9 percent—and that almost 20 percent of sixteen- and seventeen-year-olds were not enrolled—the Census Bureau had reported 10.3 percent. And even these new figures can be portrayed in a more dramatic light. Consider the following:

In one Massachusetts Census tract over 37 percent of the Puerto Rican children, aged sixteen and seventeen, were out of school. In a second Massachusetts Census tract 60 percent of sixteen- and seventeen-year-old children were out of school. Over 72 percent of the Portuguese children of that age group in that same tract were not enrolled. In a Denver, Colorado, Census tract inhabited mainly by Mexican-Americans, 12 percent of the children were out of school forty-five days or more. Complicating these findings is the number of children who have voluntarily dropped out, as compared with the number of children who, for one reason or another, have been deprived of the right to attend school.

Given the enormity of the problem of nonenrollment and absenteeism generally, it is little wonder that school districts employ people as fulltime attendance officers and aids. The job of these people is extremely important for at least two reasons. First, they possess all school attendance records and at any time are able to report the number of children absent from school. Second, attendance officers usually are the ones who contact the homes of absent children. Their inquiry and expression of concern may be the most significant factor in children returning to school.

According to the Children's Defense Fund survey, however, the number of attendance officers in each school district is typically so small, there is no way they could maintain accurate records of nonenrollment, much less contact even a tiny fraction of absent children. In Montgomery, Alabama, for example, there were, in 1973-1974, two attendance officers to oversee more than 36,000 students; Richland County, South Carolina had three attendance or home liaison workers overseeing more than 34,000 students. Davenport, Iowa, in 1973-1974, reported a total student enrollment of 23,341 and one truant officer.

While the reasons for exclusion are many, we may categorize them under three major headings:

First, children may be punished in the form of some temporary suspension for an act committed at school. While the majority of suspensions are short term, a few days or weeks, it must be remembered that the children considered in Chapter 1, where we examine school suspensions, all have been suspended for forty-five days or more.

The second major reason for exclusion is a school's lack of facilities for so-called special students, the youthful victims of the stresses caused by nature, nurture, or noxia. In Chapter 2 we consider the cases of children who bring to school such special problems as mental retardation, epilepsy, language deficiency, bed-wetting, and even pregnancy.

The third category of exclusion we have called exclusion by classification or diagnosis. Almost all schoolchildren are academically or psychologically tested. Part of the educational industry is to develop methods for determining children's capacities and incapacities, intelligence and nonintelligence, potential and lack of potential. Everyone is classified; everyone is tested. But if these processes and methods of classification were not in themselves sufficiently problematic, children are assigned to regular and so-called special classrooms according to their various test scores. In some instances, children requiring special attention do receive that attention in special education classrooms. More likely, however, special classrooms are the first stage of a child's leaving school, first for short periods of time and later forever. The child's typical excuse for such absences, if anyone bothers to ask, usually takes the form, "Nobody ever cared when I was there, so why stay?" In words familiar to all of us, exclusion by classification means testing and academic tracking. These are the topics we will consider in Chapter 3.

While these three categories adequately describe the official reasons for children being excluded from school, underlying all of them are poverty and racism. As we have noted, poor children are excluded from school far more often than middle-class and affluent children, just as minority children are excluded more often than white children. Thus, whatever the explanation given for a child's being excluded from school, an examination of the particular case usually reveals the same thing: The poor or minority child is not being given proper attention, proper care, proper education. At times this lack of attention is so blatant one cannot believe that a school is able to get away with its practice. But more subtle issues also may be at stake in the exclusion of poor and minority children, issues that may not ever become known to teachers and administrators. It is these problems that we will address in Chapter 4.

Finally, in Chapter 5, we present conclusions and recommendations for reinstating excluded children and, more generally, preventing exclusion in the first place.

The statistics speak for themselves. The number of children suspended from schools is awesome, the disproportionate numbers of minority and poor children suspended, unforgivable. But the statistics, while providing an overall accounting of the issue, also prevent us from knowing the experiences of the single child suspended from school and what he or she has been encountering. Throughout the book we have included accounts of children excluded from school, life studies as they are often called, of the people whose most urgent problems and anguish are often transformed into the very statistics we have already begun to examine.

The purpose of presenting these life studies is to convey a bit of what life is like for these people, what in personal terms exclusion from school means, and how it feels. These studies also provide us an opportunity to learn of the attitudes toward school and education generally held by those people whose voices are rarely heard. In no way should the life studies be construed as case histories. The people represented in this book have not sought psychiatric help; they are not medical cases. Their confidentiality has been preserved by supplying fictitious names.

Nothing is more precious than human experiences, especially those which tend to leave one with the feelings of shame and defeat, the feelings produced by exclusion from school. The families of children in this predicament continue to be seen in our culture as weak, sick, somehow deserving of or even creating the ill fate that has befallen them. They are, of course, anything but weak. Indeed, they reveal a special strength, one that carries them through the ordeal of school exclusion and possibly reinstatement, as well as the ordeal of living and enduring, which as Robert Coles has written, is for some the quintessential achievement.

After examining the data collected on school attendance, nonenrollment, academic performance, and intelligence scores of children in various school districts, some people continue to claim that school makes little difference in the lives of people. Send children anywhere, one hears, for what they'll become is determined by their families, not their schools, and anyway it's probably already "too late" for the child when he or she enters kindergarten.

If one is content merely to scan certain statistical reports and remain isolated from the lives of children going through school, such statements are readily made. But if one becomes implicated in the lives of children going through school or being excluded from it, if one regularly visits with these children and their families, a different story emerges, and one is less willing to utter such words. As wretched as some schools surely are, they are still seen to redeem young children, and with them their families. In the lives of poor and minority children, one rarely finds a valuable learning alternative to school. The power of school, furthermore, the experience of learning, and the significance of the myriad planes of human intelligence and competences deeply affect the evolution of a single life and the very civilization in which that life evolves, all lives evolve. It is in this real as well as spiritual context that we engage the problem of children excluded from school.

1.

Out of Work, Out of School

One is hard pressed to decide just what institution has failed America's children most. Certainly the health care and legal aid offered children is inadequate, as are the schools and the churches. The government does not underwrite the well-being of children, and economic policies rarely favor children. In a word, ours is a culture that substitutes expressions of care for actual care. Promises are made, especially during election time, but legislation, decent clinics, rehabilitation centers, jobs for young people simply do not follow.

Still, when we think about children and the single institution designed to protect them, we tend to think of schools. If a child is in school, we say almost prayerfully, he or she has a chance. Even if the child's home life is unhappy, even if the child's family lives in poverty, school just may save the child. And indeed, it often turns out that schools do precisely that. Despite ill-advised messages that schools don't matter, either academically or psychologically, those who visit schools regularly, or better, work in them, know that they can be redemptive for children.

If nothing else, school can provide a safe, calm haven for a few hours. It can provide friendships, contacts, a chance to learn some things, a chance to learn that one has worth. At least this is the hopeful side, for everyone knows that schools can also teach children that they are worthless. There are critics of education who argue that little in contemporary schools is worth keeping, the schools are that bad. More realistically, we know that America's public school system, while inadequate and harmful in many respects, is not about to be immediately transformed; the masses of children will continue to attend them, for good or for bad.

As hurtful and wasteful as some of our schools may be, the fact is that children suspended from school are liable to end up in situations far worse than had they been allowed to attend school. While many of us can leisurely debate educational issues of all sorts and design any variety of ideal educational setting, millions of children are being suspended from school and finding their already limited oportunities shrunk more, even to the point that their futures are closed by age eleven or twelve. No one can foresee what opportunities arise by dint of one's association with a school. It may be one's academic or athletic, dramatic or political talents that someday make a difference for a child; a valuable contact with someone, a favor done years ago that now can be repaid. But suspension from school can ruin it all, the talents, the contacts, the unrequited favors. The message of suspension is found in the Latin origin of the word: *suspendere*: to hang up. Suspended children are indeed hung up, in time, in space. They are prevented from learning that which school offers, they are prevented access to valuable resources, human and material. They are denied the right to develop and grow, and to live their life with the feeling that they are protected and wanted, and that the culture in the form of school teachers and administrators finds them teachable and worthy.

To say that suspension from school is a serious problem is a drastic understatement. According to a survey of over 2800 school districts conducted by the Department of Health, Education, and Welfare's Office for Civil Rights (OCR) and reported in *Children Out of School in America*, more than 1 million elementary and secondary schoolchildren were suspended at least once during the 1972-1973 school year. This number amounts to over 4 percent of the 24 million schoolchildren surveyed. Suspensions occurred in cities in the North and South, in rural districts everywhere, in large schools, in small schools. The OCR report shows that in 100 of the 580 school districts surveyed in New Jersey almost 37,000 children had been suspended in 1972-1973. In Maryland, in eighteen of the twenty-four school districts surveyed, almost 32,000 children were suspended. And in ninety-one of ninety-three South Carolina districts almost 40,000 students were suspended.

The percentages of suspended students in a particular Census tract area are equally dramatic. Census Tract 41.01 in Denver: 50 percent of white boys suspended. Census Tract 6526 in New Bedford, Massachusetts: 33 percent of black girls suspended. Sumter County, South Carolina: 36 percent of black boys suspended. Few children, it seems, escape suspension, but the figures show as well that black children are suspended more often and for longer periods of time than white children. This fact is seen in the disproportionate number of suspensions among minority students. Houston, Texas, with 56 percent minority enrollment, reported that of all suspensions, 71 percent were minority students. New York City, with 64 percent minority enrollment, reported that 86 percent of all suspensions were minority students.

The statistics are almost the same when one compares poor children, defined here as children whose families receive some sort of public assistance (like aid to dependent children), with more affluent children (those whose families do not receive public assistance). In one Macon, Georgia, Census tract, 47 percent of the children in the system came from female-headed families, but 71 percent of the suspensions were children from female-headed families. And in one Davenport, Iowa, Census tract, 29 percent of the children came from female-headed families, while 71 percent of the reported suspensions in that Census tract were from female-headed families.

The major reason offered for suspending a child from school is that the consideration of the child's case calls the parents into the deliberation, brings the parents into school. It is the reinstatement hearing, in other words, that, coupled with the seriousness of the punishment, is supposed to help the child. In fact, according to the Children's Defense Fund survey, 33 percent of suspended children are returned to school *without* their parents being involved in the reinstatement hearing. As a method of helping children, therefore, suspension hardly seems productive. Irrespective of the reinstatement process, suspensions often bring about a pattern of exclusion that leads to the termination of formal education. At first, the child is suspended, perhaps for several days—then, after a while, a second bit of trouble and a second suspension, maybe longer this time. Usually, on the occasion of the first suspension, the child is labeled by teachers and students "troublemaker," truant, "problem case." Class time is lost, the work rarely made up, and gradually the child falls away for longer and longer periods of time, until at least he or she "drops out" for good.

The stories of hundreds of thousands of children who recognize this pattern as being their own, is familiar to many. Often, within a year of the final falling away from school, children become involved in criminal activities. A recent study of the Colorado Division of Youth Services indicated that 90 percent of the 444 children in custody who were studied functioned at a mean school grade level of 4.6. Similar research in Texas showed that only 4.6 percent of 1252 children studied were at their proper educational grade level. According to a member of the Massachusetts Department of Youth Services, "98 percent of (our) children have been involved in school problems." As if the suspensions and possible criminal activities following them were not bad enough, suspended children also face the problem of the police, potential employers, and administrators of academic programs having access to their school records. This means that suspended children are marked children who may have additional difficulty finding employment or space in educational programs.

Everyday children commit acts in school that necessitate their being disciplined in some manner if some minimal order is to be maintained. In fact, some of these acts are chargeable crimes; if adults committed them, they would be criminally prosecuted. The problem, however, is that a great many of these acts, probably the majority of them, are not so severe that they warrant the child's being suspended. Furthermore, it should be obvious to school officials by now that suspensions do little to prevent the occurrence or recurrance of an undesirable act, much less help the child intellectually or emotionally.

The reasons for suspension are numerous, but according to *Children Out of School in America*, they can be categorized under five headings: first, fighting or physical contact. About 36 percent of school suspensions result from physical contact, usually between students and *rarely*, contrary to popular belief, between a student and a teacher. Granted, fighting in halls and classrooms cannot be condoned, but in the majority of cases, what is called fighting hardly merits the punishment it usually brings.

The second major category of school suspensions involves truancy and tardiness. Under this heading, which accounts for some 25 percent of school suspensions, are such familiar acts as playing hooky and cutting class. The category also includes such simple acts as leaving school a little early one afternoon and coming to school a few minutes late several mornings in a row.

About 13 percent of school suspensions are due to what might be called behavior problems. This third category includes acting out in class, "bad attitude," students disobeying teachers, and what comes down to teachers not liking students and eventually provoking students in some way. Everyone remembers the infamous class disrupters from their own schooldays, but one wonders whether most cases of so-called bad attitude warrant suspension.

Category four is verbal confrontations, specifically, insulting or disagreeing strenuously with teachers. About 10 percent of suspensions are accounted for in this category. One hears about the vicious assaults of teachers by students, stories that are often, though not always, highly exaggerated. But one hears less about the everyday argument between teacher and pupil that could end up being a valuable educational experience but that concludes instead with the student being suspended from school.

Category five is a catch-all category, including miscellaneous reasons for school suspension. Included here, however, are some of the most well-known reasons for suspension, even though these account for less than 17 percent of suspensions. The category includes smoking, destruction of property, and the highly publicized issues of dress codes, drugs, and alcohol, which in fact account for a minuscule number of suspensions. As always, violations of school ordinances on smoking and destruction of property cannot be taken lightly. But frequently the story of a suspension for destruction of property fails to coincide with what we imagine is happening in schools when we read about violence. Unfortunately, we are preoccupied with accounts of violence and destruction but remain blind to the more common acts leading to suspension.

J immy McGuinness is the second youngest of five children born to James and Estelle McGuinness. His father works on the assembly line of a small plastics factory and is in perpetual fear of losing his job. The family lives on the second floor of a three-family house. The five children occupy two bedrooms, the parents the third. The McGuinness's home, chosen primarily because of its closeness to the schools, is pleasant and a convenient five-block walk to the public grammar school all the McGuinness children have attended. The local high school is less than a mile away, and a bus runs practically from the front door of their house to the entrance of the high school.

Jimmy, an average student, was suspended from school the first time when he was in the eighth grade. The story goes that a group of boys had been milling in the hall outside the arts and crafts room when suddenly several of the boys began fighting. Jimmy was thirteen at the time, and while only four years have elapsed since then, he is barely able to recall most of the details of that incident.

"Like, I remember us there," he says, "talking about something. It must have been important to us, but I can't say now what it was all about. I remember slugging Frank Fischel. I think maybe he said something, or called my sister a name. Something. Anyway, a group of us, we was really going at it, see. I remember how crowded in we were. There wasn't no room for all of us. I didn't even see the teachers coming to break it up. All of a sudden they was just there, you know, yelling at us, telling us to report to Old Man Dryer, the assistant principal. I remember *him*. What a small time punk *he* was. He had nothing in that school to do all day *but* punish kids. He loved it if there was trouble. You could tell just by looking at him he loved it.

"He threw me out. I argued, I mean, I *tried* to argue, but he didn't let me say nothing. He just said I was fighting; there was a rule; I was out. I think like a week. Tuesday to Tuesday, something like that. Then I got sick right after that, so maybe I missed something like nine or ten days, instead of just five days like it was supposed to be. Jesus, my old man, you know, he was furious with me. And I was pissed, 'cause no one in the school never let me say nothing. I didn't *start* the fight. The guys who started it, they never got caught. It was just the rest of us. But that wasn't so bad. The bad thing was this Dryer, this pretend cop, throwing me out. He didn't let me say nothing to him in his office. Like, say the fight was at one o'clock, right? I was in my home at one-thirty. He went with me and this other guy to our lockers, stood there watching us getting our stuff, and walked us to the front door, you know, like he had to make sure we were really going. He didn't even let me see my teacher. So I missed all my work for two weeks.

"See, that was the worst part, 'cause if you ain't in school that's maybe not that bad if you keep up. I was never good in school, but I did my work. I could have done better, but I never tried. But when you throw a person out and never let him come back to get his books so's he can't do his work, then how do they expect you to keep up? I almost lost the whole year 'cause of that one lousy five-day suspension! 'Cause of that Dryer more likely."

Despite his fears that he would lose the entire year, Jimmy McGuinness was able to make up the work from his two weeks out of school. By the end of the year, as far as he was concerned, his troubles were behind him. He had passed his courses, except English, in which he had received an incomplete. His English teacher, however, was allowing him the summer months to write three compositions. When they were finished, he would pass this last course.

Less than a week into his ninth-grade year, however, it was obvious that the suspension, months before, remained a factor in the teacher's perceptions of this boy. Even some of Jimmy's fellow students reminded him of his earlier trouble and jokingly asked him what trouble he had planned for the new year. They spoke about the week in

March that Jimmy had been suspended as McGuinness Holiday week.

Jimmy took the jibes good-naturedly, but he was hurt by them. He was hurt even more when he learned from the English teacher that the incomplete could not be removed from his record until one semester had elapsed. Jimmy had handed in the three compositions, as arranged, but he now learned for the first time that he had been placed on an unofficial probation period. If he stayed out of trouble, the incomplete would be removed.

"I never thought that was fair neither. That was like not being able to tell Dryer *my* side of the story. But I went along with it. I mean, there wasn't no hurry about nothing. I could go to the high school the next year if I passed, and I did the compositions. So it was all right. It wasn't fair, like I say, but I didn't say nothing. Like, what could you say? And who could you say something to if you wanted to?

"The way I saw it, the bad part was that everybody in the school, kids too, they all had me pegged. Like, everybody was waiting around for me to get into more trouble. It's like, you know, when you go to a hockey game, and you tell people you really like to see them play, you know, but inside you're hoping there'll be a big fight? That's how it was with me that whole year. Everybody was saying they hoped I'd do okay, but, like you could sort of tell they wanted me to fall on my ass, maybe just get a little tiny suspension. If I got thrown out then they didn't have to. Lots of kids, they're always looking for trouble to brew in the schools. It's like that's what they're there for. Teachers too, especially guys like Dryer. He was always waiting for me. I don't know, maybe even my folks were waiting for trouble. They never said nothing about it, but maybe they were waiting for trouble too."

Waiting for it or not, trouble came in mid-October, some six weeks into the school year. Another scene of milling in the halls, another outbreak between boys, and this time Jimmy McGuinness was accused of pushing over some freestanding lockers, so that they blocked the entrance to the lavatories. Nine boys were suspended, but unlike the previous experience, this time each boy had an opportunity to tell Mr. Dryer and his superior, Principal Herman Ostead, their side of the story. The hearing, however, according to Jimmy, was as lopsided this year as it was the previous year. This time the boys did all the talking, Dryer and Ostead said nothing, and at the end of the two-hour session they simply announced the suspensions. First offenders—boys who had never been suspended previously—were out for one week. Jimmy and two other boys who had been suspended from the school on previous occasions were suspended for two and a half weeks. One boy,

Taggie Sheppard, who everyone reported had started the fracas, was suspended for three weeks.

Jimmy McGuinness did not receive a stern lecture from his parents as he had on the night of his first suspension. He received a beating from his father. His mother refused to hear his side of the story, or, if she listened to him, she refused to believe anything he said. She inquired of the school. Mr. Dryer himself told her the details of the fight. Mrs. McGuinness accepted the assistant principal's word.

The work that went undone during the two weeks of this second suspension was never made up. Jimmy tried. The social studies homework was barely manageable but the mathematics and science work was impossible to complete without being in class every day. At fifteen Jimmy McGuinness could see that the battle with school was over.

"I could tell. It was only a matter of how much longer. Like, I was almost fifteen, I wasn't even in the high school really. And all these people there, even my friends, they acted like I was some sort of criminal. Jesus, the way they acted around me, you'd have thought I just got out of the pen or something. Like I had a police record. The way I see it, nobody in that school was out to help anybody, which was all right, 'cause if you did work like I always *tried* to do, they'd let you get by. You had to be pretty awful dumb not to pass that school. I mean, lots of the teachers they had there, they were clowns. They had a couple of brains there, but not all that many. Some of the kids were smarter than a lot of those teachers. But they didn't help nothing by throwing me out. They knew what they were doing too. They knew when they suspended me what would happen. I'd be all through. They knew it. That's what they wanted. They got kids they think are troublemakers, they do something with them. They ain't going to keep 'em around there, getting into trouble all the time.

"In the public schools, they got to keep up. That may be all right for most of the kids, but not all of 'em. People in that school they never liked me. They wanted me out. So, how do you get a guy out? You can't flunk him if he's doing his work all right, so you wait 'til he gets into trouble then you bounce him so hard he can't never get back in. Maybe you even work on his old man and old lady a little, you know. Tell 'em their kid's a bum. If one of their friends say it, they'll bust him in the mouth. But if the school tells your old man you're no good, he'll believe 'em. Everybody believes what the school says about you. If they say you're a bum, you're a bum. They suspended you, right? Didn't let you do your work, right? So that proves you're a bum, right?"

By the end of his ninth-grade year Jimmy McGuinness had flunked two courses, science and mathematics that he had never completed during the period of his suspension. One of Jimmy's teachers wondered whether Jimmy should perhaps find a new school so that he could, in a sense, start all over again. Jimmy himself reminded the teacher what Mr. Dryer had told him: No matter what he did and where he went, the two suspensions and the incomplete courses and failures would be permanent fixtures of his school record.

"The teacher felt sorry for me. I think maybe he was the first person in all that time who really felt bad. It was like he was saying, 'you're drowning, man and I feel bad. I wish I could do something for you.' I think my old lady felt the same. She didn't like me falling out like that, but she never said nothing. The school had her believing her son was a criminal, and my old man told her I was a bum. That one teacher, he was the only nice guy in the whole lot of 'em. Talking with him, I felt sort of happy. I was dying my slow death but at least I had a guy there who was saying, 'I'm sorry. McGuinness, I'm really sorry for you. Maybe you ain't such a bad kid after all. Even with your fighting. You could pass all these courses. You ain't the dumbest kid here. You really ain't. We've had dumber kids here than you.'"

Jimmy McGuinness was smiling as he continued to imagine what this one teacher, his single friend in the school, might have been thinking. "'We've had dumber kids in the school before. I can't remember any off hand, but we must have had *somebody* dumber.'"

Perhaps the most remarkable part of the suspension stories was that Jimmy McGuinness's personality made one think that he would never involve himself in fights, especially in school where everyone knew the consequences of fighting. He was neither moody nor mercurial. Indeed, his temperament seemed even. If anything, he was a vulnerable boy, someone who seemed to be walking through life incredulous that events, like the suspensions, could befall him. His brothers were not unlike him. Whereas his father often revealed a fiery temperament, the boys rarely did, even when they were pushed by their friends to the point when many young people would bust out and start brawling. Something about school had the effect of lowering this one boy's boiling point.

During the middle of April in his last year in grammar school, Jimmy McGuinness saw some boys and girls tussling in the schoolyard one day after school. Again, the details of the incident are unclear. Someone said the students were only teasing one another. Some said they were engaging in sexual activities. One of the girls involved in the incident said a boy was trying to have sex with his girlfriend, who was unable to resist. She said that Jimmy had come to her rescue, even though he barely knew the girl. A door leading to a hallway outside the gymnasium got broken, as did several windows. All the students were suspended. At the time of the incident, all the students ran away except one boy who turned himself in and reported the names of everyone he could remember being there. Some of the students were given a warning by the administration, others received more drastic punishment. For the third time Jimmy McGuinness was suspended.

The suspension was to last one week. Upon returning to school he began cutting classes. He was absent nearly half of the month of May. By June he stopped going to school altogether. Amazingly, he was graduated from grammar school and entered high school the following autumn. He attended his high school classes irregularly, after pledging to his family that he would do his best to stay in school. By Christmas of his first year in high school he had dropped out for good. No one in the school ever inquired about him. A letter was written to his parents, but he never saw it. There was no remonstration from his parents, merely the order to find a job.

"I don't see, like, what I done as quitting school," he said, after being out of school one year. "The way I see it, they quit on *me* first. First the school, then my parents. If they hadn't quit, I'd still be there. There was a guy I know, we went to grammar school together. He was suspended like me once, and it scared the hell out of him. He went off the wall, he was so scared. I never felt that way. I knew they'd let me back in, but this guy was really out of it. So then his homeroom teacher called him up, while he was suspended, you know. The lady just called him up on the telephone, maybe like two, three times. Just to see how he was. He never forgot it. He was never suspended again neither. He had someone looking out for him, someone who was worried whether he was going to be all right.

"I always thought, if one person in the world had called me up, from the school I mean, to say hello. All they had to do is say, hello, go to hell, McGuinness, I'd have been better off. I might have stayed in too. But no one gave a damn. No one calling to see whether you're okay, just to find out even whether you're still alive—makes you think you're not a worthwhile person, you know what I mean? If I got one thing out of those suspensions, it was that I was a guy without any worth in the world. Like I was a dollar bill, you know—no one was using those kind of dollar bills no more. I mean it. One phone call, even from that guy Dryer, and I might still be in there now. When you just go and suspend a kid, all you're doing is saying get the hell out of here, kid, and don't come back 'til we tell you to. And even when it's all right to come back, they still don't want you. You're still the wrong kind of a dollar."

The pain of the suspension and his final dropping out hadn't subsided before still a new problem confronted him. On his first four attempts to gain employment, he was thwarted by personnel people who referred to his record of suspensions. All four people had contacted his high school and been advised of his three suspensions. They couldn't take a chance with him, not with a record like his. A fifth job opened up thanks to a friend who convinced Mr. Thomas Garrity that he could use Jimmy in his small grocery store. Tom Garrity told Jimmy he was hiring him, suspensions and all, for two dollars an hour, but that Jimmy should think of the first several months of the job as a probation period. Jimmy's performance on the job was faultless, and he remains in the employ of Tom Garrity.

There has been no trouble now for many months. Jimmy McGuinness's parents are content with their son. There is no contact between the school and the McGuinness family. There is talk about Jimmy's returning to school sometime, although he realizes that the chances of it happening are reduced each day that he remains out of school.

"I ain't the first to quit. Won't be the last neither. Lots of kids drop out. Most of 'em are poor, like me, but rich ones too, they quit. The way I see it, though, the suspension, that first time, that was the one that set it up for me bad. From then on it was a pattern. Maybe I got into trouble 'cause I wanted attention. Maybe that's the answer; I don't know. All I know is that no one in school cared nothing about what I did or didn't do. Sure, I dropped out. But if you go back and really look at my case, they really pushed me out. They never once tried to help me. They didn't once care if I dropped behind in my work or got bad grades after they suspended me. They never once came after me when I started cutting. They probably told the truant officers, if you find the guy, forget it. We don't want him back.

"And another thing. They're following me around everywhere I go with that suspension. I try to get a job—no way. 'You're suspended kid. No one who gets suspended gets a job here.' Special classes at that night school place, *they* even wanted to give me static. You know what I am, man? I'm an ex-con who's never even been in prison. That's the way they see me, like an ex-con. I got suspended, right? So it's like I got this scar on my face that says nobody can touch me or talk to me or give me a job, 'cause I've been suspended. Hell, a real ex-con who finished school, maybe even in prison, he'll get a job faster than I will, and he's maybe knocked off some gas station or broke into a store. All I done was fight once or twice in the school. I'm worse off than that guy by far. Prison helped him out, but my school wouldn't help me out. If that's what this country calls fair, then I'll eat it.

"They killed me, my school. They killed me like with a gun. Bam, right between the eyes. Those suspensions follow me everywhere. Probably keep me out of a cemetery someday when I die, 'cause I got suspended. 'Don't want to have no guy who's been suspended lying on the same ground with all these other people who finished school now, do we?' That school killed me. They *thought* all they were doing was throwing me out for five, ten days at a time. They didn't know they were driving the nails into my coffin. Schools could help out too. They could really help out. But they don't want to. It's just easier to let people like me fall away. That's what they do too. First we fall away, then we crawl away . . . Then we're dead."

Madelon Northrup turned sixteen in July. Over the summer she worked in a restaurant near her home in Boston's Roxbury district. She assisted in the kitchen and cleaned up after closing. Most of the money she earned went to her parents; she was able to keep a few dollars each week for herself. Although the job was uninteresting and there were times she wished she could quit, she comforted herself with the knowledge that when school reopened in September she would be working in the restaurant only three nights a week and Saturday afternoons. School was bad, she told herself, but it beat washing dishes and dragging barrels of garbage into the alley on sweltering hot nights. Anyway, they should have hired a boy to do most of the jobs she was made to do.

In August any thoughts Madelon might have had of stopping work ended abruptly. Her father had lost his own job and now the only money the Northrups had coming in was being earned by her mother Cecile, who worked as a maid in a Boston hotel, and her brother Jo-Henry, who found parttime jobs in service stations around the neighborhood.

Dalton Northrup was infuriated and ashamed by being out of work. The whole story of his life, he said again and again, was unemployment. "Ain't a question of people holding jobs anymore," he shouted at his wife and mother one night. "It's a question of whether they're going to give us *any* jobs. Here they go giving it to you one day and pulling it back the next. How they expect a man to make a living? It don't pay to be honest. Whole country's set up to turn people into criminals. How else you supposed to make a dollar but snatch it off your brother out there on the sidewalk?"

No amount of consoling could lessen his anger. He was embarrassed that his wife was earning more than he and by the prospect of the family going on welfare.

Cecile urged him to borrow money from their older sons who had steady jobs, but at forty-six, Dalton Northrup was not about to live off his children. "Money coming into the house is supposed to be earned by *me*, not by no twenty-year-old boys. When a man can't do it, he might as well die. Not a damn thing in the world no more for me to be proud of."

When Cecile went to bed, Dalton's mother, sixty-four-year-old Joetta Northrup, spoke to her son with sternness in her voice. She told him he had better borrow money from anybody he could, because the money the family was bringing in now wasn't going to keep them going another month. There was food to be bought no matter how high the prices went, and winter clothes to get, and rent, and something he didn't know about, Cecile's hysterectomy, an operation that had been put off too many times. "It had to be done soon otherwise she might get cancer for sure," Joetta told him. "May already be too late."

Dalton was shocked. "She going to die of cancer?"

"If she don't get that operation she will."

"She never told me," he said softly.

"Didn't tell no one. I heard her talking to the doctor on the telephone. She doesn't suspect I know anything."

There were many more conversations that summer, mostly at night when the older Northrups thought that Madelon and Jo-Henry were asleep. But the children were awake, listening to every word and becoming increasingly frightened by the thought of having no money and their mother dying of cancer, which in fact was not true. Yet, as no one talked about Cecile's operation, no one knew the severity of her illness.

In late August Dalton borrowed three hundred dollars from his sons. They offered him more, but he assured them he would be able to land a job soon. He gave most of the money to his wife. The remainder they put away in a jar; it was to be their private savings. They would use it only if a real emergency arose. Madelon continued working, extra hours too, whenever possible. Overtime pay netted her eight extra dollars a week. The temptation to hang around with her friends was great, but the image of her father's anguish and her mother's illness turned aside any temptations.

In September jmadelon and Jo-Henry returned to school. Then one evening Dalton announced that he had found a job. To celebrate he took Cecile out drinking. The children stayed home with their grandmother. For the first time in months, the family was happy, hopeful even. Best of all, there were no arguments to keep the children awake.

The next morning Madelon awoke early as she always did, to fix breakfast for the family. She found her father fully dressed, asleep on the living room floor. Cecile had returned early in the evening, leaving Dalton at a bar with some friends. There was no job. Dalton's behavior that night turned out to be only the beginning. Soon he was going out earlier in the day and coming home barely able to stand up. At first Cecile and Joetta let him alone, believing it all right for a man as desperate as Dalton was to get drunk. But after a while, they could tolerate it no longer.

The sight of her father staggering around the apartment, mumbling words she could not understand and swearing as he had never done, frightened Madelon. She felt nervous almost all the time, and at night, on returning from the restaurant exhausted, she could not fall asleep. She felt sorry for both her parents but angry with them, too, for not being able to change things. Her father could get a job, she told herself, if he really wanted.

Jo-Henry disagreed. It was "too damn hard for black men to find jobs in this city," he said; what was happening to their dad was happening to thousands of men all around. But Madelon continued to believe people can do something for themselves. "Anyway, only weak people drink," she argued with her brother.

"You mean people are made weak by not working," Jo-Henry corrected her. "He ain't no weak man. He's one of the strongest men I've ever seen," he said proudly.

Madelon was not persuaded. Her anger and confusion increased, making it more difficult for her to do her school work. She looked forward to the hours in the restaurant, for the physical work seemed to quiet her thoughts.

Cecile entered the hospital for her operation in late September. Before leaving the apartment she explained the reasons for the operation to Madelon. Joetta sat with them. Jo-Henry was at work.

"You scared, Mama?" Madelon asked.

"Nothing to be scared of," Cecile laughed. "Lots of women have this operation. They do it almost automatically. Nothing serious to it at all."

"You going to be sick later on from it?"

"I'll feel like *hell* for a couple of days, then I'll be fine."

"But I mean after that?" Madelon wondered, looking at her grandmother.

"You thinking I'm going to die, Madelon? I ain't going to die. You don't die from operations, you're supposed to *live* from them. At least that's what I'm hoping you do." She smiled. "I ain't planning on not coming back. Not this time anyway. I may be no good now to have children, but I ain't too old to be a grandmother."

Joetta grinned and nodded her head. "Don't you go saying nothing about grandmothers, now," she teased. The two women laughed, and Madelon felt relieved. Before going to sleep, she listened at the bedroom door to see whether her mother would mention something that she hadn't wanted her daughter to hear. Nothing was said.

In the morning Madelon helped her mother get ready to go to the hospital. A friend of the family's would drive her, since Dalton had stayed out all night. Cecile said nothing about it. She kissed her daughter goodbye and told her she would call her from the hospital to arrange a visiting time.

On the way to school Madelon began to cry. The fear of her mother going to the hospital and her anger at her father for not being at home overwhelmed her. She arrived at school late, having totally forgotten about the examination in first period English. Unprepared, she answered only one of the five questions. She pretended to write a great deal so that the teacher would not know how poorly she had done until later.

In the lunch line waiting to buy milk, she was unable to think of anything but her mother's operation and her father lying drunk somewhere. Suddenly she was accidentally pushed by another girl. The push became an argument, the argument a fight. Madelon slapped at the girl and got back a punch in the side of her head. Then they were pulling at each other and swearing and hitting. A cafeteria official tried to stop them by pushing herself in between the girls, but Madelon knocked her away and swore at her. Finally a policeman and two men teachers separated the girls, who hurled names at one another and wrestled to get free.

Within the hour Madelon was seated across the desk from an

assistant principal. The man asked for Madelon's story. She told him what happened. "Did she know," he asked, "that she had pushed a school official and called her putrid names?" Madelon knew the woman was an official, but the fight was going on and she couldn't stop herself. "So you knew," he repeated, "exactly what you were doing when you did it?"

"I couldn't do anything about it," she replied. "Everybody would have done like I did."

"Two more questions," he said in an accusatory tone. "First thing I want to know is how you are doing in school?"

"Okay," she answered flatly.

"Except you flunked an English test this morning, didn't you? And two mathematics tests last week. In other words, what *you* think is good is actually flunking."

Madelon had not learned the results of the mathematics tests and was surprised that the English teacher had already graded her examination.

"Number two," the assistant principal continued, "is there anything going on at home that we should know about? Several teachers have noted a change in you from last year, and I don't have to hide the fact that it's not for the good. Kids like you are always finding trouble. *That* we can't stop, but is there anything at home going on as well?"

Madelon sat still in the chair and looked at the administrator. She thought of telling him about her mother's operation and her father's drinking. But as she was about to speak, something her father once told her and Jo-Henry suddenly returned. Just before entering high school—Jo-Henry had finished his first year·—Dalton Northrup took his son and daughter on a Sunday walk in the small park behind the church near their home.

"Before you start in this new school of yours," he told Madelon, "I want to tell you something you better never forget. There are going to be all sorts of folks in your school wanting to know about you and your brothers and your mother and me. Your grandmother too, probably. They're going to ask you all kinds of questions. Like, how we're doing. How rich or poor we are. I don't want you telling these people nothing. You understand? Nothing. What we're doing outside of that school is nobody's business. Especially those principals. Those guys make trouble for families like us. They spend more time reporting welfare violations than teaching. So if the time ever comes when one of those men starts asking his questions, you just remember that you don't have to answer him."

"You have something to tell me, Madelon?" the assistant principal asked, beginning to lose his patience.

"Everything in my family is real fine, Mr. Crampton. Real fine. Honest."

"Well then, your folks ought to be pretty upset when they hear about this." The administrator could see the girl becoming nervous at the thought of her parents learning of her difficulty. "Come see me tomorrow. Before you go to lunch."

At home that night Madelon said nothing of the fight or the talk with the assistant principal. Her mother's operation had gone well. Madelon could visit her the next day. Her father ate dinner without speaking. It was clear that he was sick. He went to bed as soon as he finished eating. Washing the dishes, Madelon heard him in the bathroom trying to vomit.

The next day Mr. Crampton met Madelon at the door of his office. "You don't need to come in," he said. "We're going to suspend you from school for one week. You go home now and come back one week from tomorrow. Then you're on probation for the next month. You get into trouble during that time, and we'll be a whole lot tougher on you."

"Yes sir."

"You have any questions?"

"Do I go to eat lunch or do I go home now?"

"I think you just better go home now. Anybody at your home?"

"Yes sir, my grandmother."

"Then she'll let you in."

"Does this mean I can't work at my job?"

"Has nothing to do with anything outside of school. Outside of here we have nothing to say about how you lead your life. That's your business."

Joetta was deeply upset by the suspension, but she and Madelon kept the secret well hidden from Cecile when they visited her that afternoon at the hospital. When Dalton learned of the fight and the suspension he flew into a rage. He yelled at his daughter for misbehaving and threatened to whip her. Then he turned his anger at the school. He wanted to know the assistant principal's name, promising he would visit the man first thing next morning. Then Dalton resigned himself to waiting.

The next morning at school he demanded an explanation of the punishment. Told that fighting a school official was the worst offense a student could commit, Dalton retorted that the assistant principal sounded more like a judge than a teacher. He argued that the school had no right to throw the girl out for even one minute, and he refused Mr. Crompton's request that he leave. Dalton was advised that a policeman would throw him out, if he didn't leave at once.

"Go get your big policeman then," Dalton shouted at the assistant principal. "What do you got here anyway, a jail?"

"Don't you have to go to work?" Mr. Crampton asked contemptuously.

"None of your business when I go to work."

"*Do* you work, Mr. Northrup?"

"Of course I work. All men have to work, except for guys who spend their time throwing little girls out of school."

"So why aren't you working this morning?"

"Because I work the night shift. You ever hear of working a night shift?"

"Of course."

"Mister, I'm getting sorrier and sorrier that my daughter didn't sock *you* instead of that other little girl."

"I'm beginning to see where your daughter gets her problems from."

"What the hell's that supposed to mean?"

Before the principal could respond, a policeman appeared in the corridor and stood inside the entrance to the principal's office.

"Get him out of here, Walter," Mr. Crampton ordered. "Mr. Northrup is only making things worse for his daughter." The policeman took Dalton's arm, but Dalton shook it free and headed toward the door. "You might be interested to know, Mr. Northrup," the administrator was saying, "that I asked your daughter how things were going at home. You know what she said? She said things were fine. Absolutely fine."

Dalton smiled. Outside in the hall, he looked with puzzlement at the policeman, a black man of almost his age. "What the hell you doing, man? You *working* for them or something? You ain't on their side too, are you?"

Dalton did not come home that night. Madelon heard from a girlfriend of her father's argument with the assistant principal. It was the best fight anyone ever had with Mr. Crampton, she was told, and the first time anyone ever challenged the procedure of suspension. Cecile, however, was not proud of Dalton's performance. She was infuriated by the suspension and worried that her husband's anger would only upset Madelon. After being home several days she still felt too weak to visit the school. Her inquiries would have to be made after the suspension period had ended. Perhaps it was best, as Joetta said, that everything be forgotten. Madelon would behave, and there would be no more trouble.

"You got scared when I went to the hospital, didn't you?" Cecile asked her daughter.

Madelon nodded.

"Between that and your father's drinking you were really all set to be a good student, weren't you?" She stroked Madelon's cheek.

"I forgot an English test."

"You're lucky you didn't forget your name. Where the hell is he, anyway, Joetta?" Cecile asked her mother-in-law.

"I don't know," the older woman sighed. "I don't know. But he's breaking these two kids. He's going to break us all in half if he's not careful."

"School's going to break me," Madelon mumbled under her breath.

"You're going to work, that's all," her mother encouraged her. "You'll work and get right back where you're supposed to be. Then you'll *have* to behave yourself. Every time somebody starts something, you'll just back away. Hear?"

Madelon nodded. Joetta was nodding too.

"Your daddy whip you?" Cecile asked.

"I thought he was going to, but he didn't."

"Well, that's one good thing. Being suspended is whipping enough if you ask me. We've had one week, haven't we, daughter? White doctors taking half my insides out, white principals keeping you from going to school. And we got a father running around drinking. Where's Jo-Henry?"

"He's working," Joetta answered quickly, making certain to have any good news heard.

"You been working at the restaurant, Madelon?"

"All the time."

"Overtime too, I'll bet."

"All eight dollars," Madelon muttered.

"Add 'em up, child. They count. We got any money left in our jar?" No one answered her. The money Cecile and Dalton had put away as their special savings was spent weeks ago. "This one family," she sighed, "has got itself one very long list of problems. I think I'm sorry I ever got myself operated on. Maybe I ought to go back there and have them put my parts back in and get my money back." Nobody laughed. "It was the wrong time, Joetta. I told you that right from the beginning. This whole family's going through a wrong time."

Dalton Northrup had still not found steady work by November. His drinking had lessened slightly, but his rage had not receded. Arguments were a daily event. The money he continued to borrow from his sons with no hope now of paying back only symbolized his sense of failure. Cecile, in the meantime, was not healing as well as her doctor would have liked. Two nights she awakened with severe pain and hemorrhaging, once so heavily that the police took her back to the hospital.

Madelon was more distressed than before. She was convinced her father was about to leave home for good. Talk of the family's running out of money, her mother's illness, her father's drinking, the fights and their effect on Joetta, who seemed to be aging so quickly, made it impossible for her to concentrate on schoolwork. She was trying drugs and enjoying the moments of peace they afforded her. Her course work was going badly, and she had taken to copying other people's homework and even cheating on examinations. More than anything, she feared that if she flunked, it would destroy her family forever. Frightened to say anything, she refused help from a young teacher who had substituted in the school for several days and taken a liking to Madelon. They met once, and the woman asked about her parents. Madelon described the situation at home. She told the teacher of her mother's illness and her father's unemployment and drinking. She even admitted to taking drugs. Then she felt badly that she had confessed these things. The two did not meet again, although the woman urged Madelon to let her visit the Northrups' apartment. Madelon wanted to see the woman but could not get herself to face anybody, especially at home.

A week before the Christmas holiday, Madelon's mathematics teacher notified Mr. Crampton that Madelon and four other students had been cheating on homework assignments and tests. Once again she was called to the principal's office. All five students were suspended for two weeks. Madelon was advised she could have gotten extra time because of the fight in September but that they had decided to be lenient. The students were to return to school in the third week of January, when they could attempt to make up the work they had lost and redo all the assignments on which they had cheated.

Madelon staqed after the others were dismissed. "Why didn't you keep working with that substitute woman when you had the chance?" Mr. Crampton asked her. She could not answer him. "You had a perfect chance. What, do you like getting in trouble?"

Trembling with fear, she shook her head.

"What's the matter with you black kids, don't you want to have anything to do with white teachers? You really think they're *all* out to get you or something?"

Madelon cried, stood up, and began to leave the office.

"I haven't excused you yet, young lady. I asked you a question. What have you got against white teachers?"

"Please, can't I go?" she cried.

"All right," he gave in, "go. Go wherever the hell you kids go. But don't let me hear you or any of your friends, or your father blaming this school. You had a lot of chances this year. More than you'd get at most schools. You better tell that to your parents, before they come in here with their sob stories—especially your father. What is he, anyway, some kind of a wrestler or something? He's a pretty angry guy isn't he?"

"I want you to die," Madelon whispered as she descended the stairs to the main floor. "I want everybody here to die." She was still crying when she reached her home. There was no way to hide the suspension from her family. She had spoiled their lives. There was nothing anyone could do. She hadn't caused their troubles in the beginning, but now she had made it impossible for things to get better. Jo-Henry would yell at her, and her father would beat her this time, for sure. Even Joetta would not accept the cheating. Madelon thought of never seeing her family again. The year was wasted; she would have to make up all her courses, which would mean she would be a sophomore again next year. And maybe the year after that too.

She walked slowly up the stairs of the apartment building. The stairhall was barely warmer than outside. Joetta and her mother would be home. It would be cold in the apartment, and she would be afraid to ask for anything to eat since she was supposed to be at school. They would question her, wondering why she was unable to do her work like all the other students, some of whom were worse off than she. But no one would question the school's decision. They had to do it, someone would say. Schools cannot run without rules; students have to obey the rules or pay the price. Even Jo-Henry would side with them against her. After all, the school warned everybody time and time again about cheating, and fighting, and smoking in the lavatories. She had no one to blame, just like the principal had said.

Suddenly Madelon turned and bolted down the stairs. The kids would be at the restaurant or at Pickney's house or near the filling station on Wentworth. They would have things to do, and there would be no discussions about school and suspensions and repeating grades.

She could return at night, for supper, or after supper, or tomorrow night and talk with her mother. She pushed the front-hall door open and ran down the outside steps to the street. It was beginning to snow. She glanced up at the windows on the fourth floor, but no one was up there watching her. Staying out like the old man, she thought. Anyway, it would be easier to talk later on, like tomorrow night. It was just easier at night.

When Sadao Fujimitsu was a baby, his uncle decided to call him Yoshi. The name stuck firmly in the Fujimitsu family but not in school. There, from the time he started kindergarten, Sadao was called Teddy for reasons no one seems to remember. Suddenly he was Teddy, and because the school he attended had very few Japanese Americans, the name Fujimitsu also got lost somewhere along the line. The other children called him Teddy Fudge, Fudge Cake, Hot Fudge.

At first, so his parents say, everyone laughed at these various names. His father, Rynosue, who was born in Hawaii and came to the mainland shortly before Sadao's birth, chose to believe that the new names his son was given in school were indications of his being accepted by his classmates. His mother Linda Kitagawa, who was born in Los Angeles and met her husband on a trip to Hawaii, was always disturbed by the names her son brought home. "If they want to be his friend," I have heard her say, "then they should call him by his real name. If he wants to be known as Fudge Cake, that's all right. But in this house he is Sadao. Maybe Yoshi too. It is a fine name, and the other children should learn it and use it. You do not communicate with anybody when you refuse to call them by their true name. That is the mistake Americans have always made. They think they're making everyone equal by giving them names like Dick and Bill and Teddy. But all they're doing is turning people away. If you ask Sadao, he'll tell you what name he prefers. He won't really talk to anybody who calls him by any other name. They think he's their friend, but he isn't. He's only pretending to be."

In the years that I had visited with the Fujimitsu family, I had never gotten the sense that Sadao cared that much what I called him. He did remark once that while my Japanese pronunciation stunk, he was nonetheless impressed that I remembered his name after hearing it only once. "It's a familiar name, Sadao," I told him, "because it's also the first name of a great Japanese printmaker." Sadao looked at me, his face showing puzzlement. "Sadao Watanabe," I explained. "He does gorgeous prints, usually on themes from the Bible."

"Oh yeah?" Sadao made certain not to compliment me on my knowledge, but he could not conceal his pride. He was twelve at the time, and Japanese artifacts and art objects meant a great deal to him, even the pieces he called cheap. His eyes grew large the first time I took him to one of the local art museums and showed him the galleries of Oriental art. Almost at once he fell in love with some statues in high glass cases, although his expression fell when I told him that the pieces were Chinese. Still, that they were made in the seventh century impressed him. "Where's the Japanese stuff?" he asked impatiently. We began reading the labels on the cases, figures and vases, Sadao shouting out, "Here's another one," each time he located a Japanese piece.

It was a perfect afternoon. Sadao walked out of the museum holding so tightly to the postcards we had purchased, one would have thought he had the actual treasures in his hand rather than mere photographs of them. Coming home on the trolley from the museum, Sadao was suddenly eager to talk to me.

"There aren't any Japanese people in my school," he said. "Just a few students, you know. But nobody old. They have everybody else there, but they don't have Japanese people. Usually I don't think about it. They have you doing so many things you don't have time to think about it. But every once in a while I'll think, what if I ever get into some real trouble? Who they going to make me talk to? If they had one principal or one teacher, then I could talk to him if I got in trouble, but now I have to wait until I get home. And another thing. Sometimes it's good to be able to speak Japanese with somebody. We do at home all the time. My father's worried that his children are going to grow up speaking only English and forget Japanese. I don't really think about it but I'm glad we speak it. Every once in a while I'll speak it with one of my friends, you know, and everybody tries to listen to us. You should see, they get real mad that they can't understand us. Just 'cause you're talking with words they can't understand they think you have to be talking about *them*." Sadao began to laugh. "It's true too. Sometimes we *are* speaking about them. Like, with some boy we don't like, if we want to get him angry we'll speak Japanese. They really hate that. 'Tell us, man. Tell us what you're saying.' That's what they do. It would bother me to hear them talk some language I don't understand too, but they don't know how it feels to be the guy who's always different from everybody else. I don't feel anything when I speak with my mother and father at home. But when I speak at school, and I know the other kids don't know what I'm saying, I feel strong. Like I'm bigger than they are. Not better, you know, but bigger."

"Would you like them to call you by your real name?" I asked.

"If I had a choice, they'd call me Sadao."

"And they'd say it exactly the way you say it, right?"

"Sure." He was sitting up straight on the trolley car bench. "They could learn to say it the right way. Heck, I learned how to say their names the right way. I don't call them Fudge Cake or Candy Man."

"What do the teachers call you?"

"Teddy," he mumbled.

"Teddy Fujimitsu," I said mostly to myself.

"Usually it's just Teddy F. Like, when they do the roll they go, 'Fitzsimmons, Freemont, Friliporte, Teddy F.' Some of them say Fujimitsu, but usually not until we've been in school a while. In the beginning they try to say it, but they always mess it up."

"The kids laugh?"

Sadao looked down at the rubber mats on the trolley car floor. He held tightly to the small bag containing his postcards. He didn't answer my question.

Perhaps the word that best characterizes Sadao Fujimitsu is constant. Although he has changed in the years that I have known him, there remains a steadfast and consistent way about him. Children recognize it too. Those his age as well as younger go to him to settle disputes or receive special encouragement. It is not that he is any grand arbitrator, someone able to resolve other people's trials without becoming involved with friends himself. He simply is constant, trustworthy.

It is a rare quality, his teachers have remarked, because it is often associated with less creative people. Somehow we think of the creative personality as being unpredictable, impulsive, mercurial. Whether this is more than an impression one cannot say, but Sadao was both constant and creative. His drawings and constructions were splendid, his ability to repair old things and design new ones in the wood shop, remarkable. Linguistically, too, he was outstanding. He wrote poetry, even invented words, and somewhere along the line developed a talent for helping children learn to read. Frequently after school he visited a day-care center near his home and worked with children four and five years old. I accompanied him several times and watched a group of children read from a book that they passed about. Sadao looked up at me as if to say, you didn't believe I could teach them, did you? I grinned at him and shook my head. The women supervising the children paid no attention to Sadao. They treated him as though he were a member of their staff. The children loved him and learned from him.

After my first visit to the day care center Sadao spoke about his interest in children and the business he was thinking of starting.

"When you know two languages, learn them at the same time, like I did, words mean something special to you. It's easier to read, or it was for me. It's no problem teaching little kids to read. I could do it. Japanese or English. Either one." When I suggested that it might be good to teach some children Japanese Sadao laughed out loud. "Sure and have their mothers calling my mother every night. 'Mrs. Fujimitsu,'" he mimicked an imaginary caller, "'your horrible son is teaching my child Japanese. He's got them sitting on the floor in our day care center with paper and a brush making strange letters. And Mrs. Fujimitsu, they do not go across the paper, they go up and down. Or down and up. Nobody can read what they're writing. What is your son doing to our children? We must stop him at once. We'll call the police.' Can you see my mother talking to that other lady? She's got this little Spanish kid, and I'm trying to teach him Japanese. I think I better stick with English."

"You're absolutely great at it, Sadao," I complimented him again.

"I was thinking maybe I'd start a business. Teach kids to read. Only English though." He grinned. "I could do it. I could get, like, six kids in a group and do two groups every afternoon. An hour each. Kids can't take more than that. Probably thirty minutes is all they'd be ready for. Maybe charge them fifty cents. So I get like three dollars a group, six dollars a day. Heck, I could do it three days a week and make eighteen dollars!"

We were sitting on a stone bench in the middle of a playground near his house. Sadao watched the few children running about, but he was concentrating on his new ideas. "I'd like to help little kids. I might do it when I get old too. For real. Some kids I know, they say they're going to be doctors or teachers, engineers maybe, but I'd like to work with little kids. Sports and art and reading. Little kids need a lot of attention. If you watch them a lot, they like to be with grown-ups, but they'd rather be with kids a little bit older. Like, they'll listen to their parents, but they'd rather be with their brothers and sisters. Not the brother or sister who's just a little bit older than they are, but the one a little bit older than that. The kids at the center think of me as their older brother. That's why they like me. They know I'm no grown-up, so they're not afraid. Anyway, they got grown-up women there when they need them. That's another thing. Children grow up and never see any men in school, except some of the coaches and principals. But no one has anything to do with the principals unless they get in trouble. So that's why I'd like to work with children too. I could teach them all sort of things. You remember that light I made?"

I nodded yes and let him see in my expression how impressed I was by it. When he was eleven, Sadao constructed a long snakelike column out of paper. It must have been five feet in length. All along the column he had cut out openings of various shapes and then glued colored paper around the openings in such a way that an ingenious design was formed. Then he strung two lights inside the column, doing a masterful job of hiding the wire. The result was a handsome lamp that now hangs from the ceiling of his parents' living room. When one pushes it, the light appears to jump because the various color patches light up throughout the column. It took Sadao a month to finish it.

"I could teach children to make lights like that in a short time," he was saying. "I even got a way to gt all the paper I need. In fact I've been working on a plan to use newspaper for that, maybe stiffening it with glue so that it feels like construction paper. Then you could have the kids paint it or glue stuff they find in garbage cans on it. Like broken glass and pieces of wood. Stuff like that would really look great with all the light coming through. I'd have to file down the glass for them, so they wouldn't cut themselves. Then I'd do all the wiring. You can't let little kids do that. They'd probably electrocute themselves before they even plugged it in. I think I know a place where I could get small light bulbs. Bigger than Christmas tree bulbs but not any big 100 watt-ers, or something like that."

I think of conversations like these when I want to picture Sadao Fujimitsu in my mind. There is always an energy about him. He has his school and after-school projects, his endless plans, and everything is said and executed in an artistic manner. He is all boy, everyone sees this, but there is a manliness about him as well. He can be bold as well as shy, assertive as well as quietly compliant. Yet in his work he is constant and reliable, though not predictable. One never knows what new ideas he might scheme overnight or what new projects he may be deciding to undertake.

I especially enjoy watching Sadao work. He is an exceptional teacher, always explaining what he does and how one step fits into some overall plan. His coordination is marvelous and from his mother,

I suppose, he has inherited grace. He does most of his creative work in the basement of the tenement building in which the Fujimitsus live. The landlord, Mike Tajima, is a friend of the family's, so close a friend in fact that he is called uncle. Admiring Sadao and treating him as if he were his own son, Mike Tajima turned a part of the basement into a studio for Sadao. He built shelves and tables, strung lights across the low ceiling and painted the room with bright colors. On the basement door he wrote, STUDIO, PROPERTY OF SADAO FUJIMITSU. Below this, in Japanese he painted the word "LUCK."

I remember sitting with Sadao once in his studio watching him construct what he called a bathroom collage. He had brought down a sample of every product he could find in the family bathroom. Toothpaste tubes, shave cream, bath oils, medicine, soap, towels, tissue, deodorant was piled around him as he kneeled before a rectangular piece of masonite on which he had painted a rich abstract design. Deftly he applied materials to the board blending their colors and textures with the paint beneath them. The effect was dazzling, so were the smells, a feature of the work that at times made us laugh. Sadao, of course, had to do a bit of clowning, like spray me with deodorant and feign an attack with shave cream. In the process he spilled a large glob on the floor. Becoming serious, his hand swooped down and rather than pick up the glob he slid the heel of his hand along the floor in such a way that the entire glob came up and swept the floor dry in one motion. Without stopping, he carefully applied the shave cream to the masonite as if the spill had not been an accident at all. I was thrilled by the beauty of his motion, but Sadao was unconscious of his own choreography.

I mention this recollection because, like our conversations, it represents the graceful elegance and sensuous movement of this boy. It shows, I think, what his friends know to be true, that Sadao's actions and gestures are kindly ones, lyrical and free, never harsh or abrupt. I have never heard a loud voice in the Fujimitsu household, and I have been present when tempers were high. But the flowing soft motion of the family continued and their graceful carriage, even among the youngest children, was maintained. I mention this too, because it stands in sharp contrast to an episode in school that happened a short time ago.

Apparently Sadao was speaking to a friend when a teacher called the class to order. It was not, he claimed, a purposeful attempt to interrupt the class; he was so involved in his conversation he failed to hear the teacher. Finally, the teacher yelled at him to shut up, mispronouncing

Fujimitsu in the process. Humiliated and angered, Sadao said nothing. The teacher could see that the boy was ashamed but rather than discuss the problem after class he approached Sadao in the hall where several students were talking. Not being there I am uncertain what, exactly, was said, but the teacher acknowledged that he challenged Sadao's sensitivity and inability to be disciplined or admonished. Sadao remained silent while the students watched intently, waiting for the explosion they knew would have to come.

Months before the teacher had learned that Sadao had told another teacher that he felt the people in his school should not laugh at his name. He was willing to be called Teddy, he had said, but they had to learn to pronounce Fujimitsu. They had to say it, moreover, without making a joke. Until this moment, nothing had been mentioned about Sadao's request, but now the teacher wanted to retaliate.

Again he challenged Sadao, raising the issue of the boy's talking in class, his goody-goody ways, his too-perfect record in the school, his immaculate appearance. Sadao still refused to speak, but his eyes, the students reported, were gleaming mad. They had never seen Sadao as angry. Taunting him, the teacher began walking slowly toward Sadao, needling him about his feeling ashamed that he could ever make a mistake, like talking in class. Sadao only retreated and clenched his fists. The teacher persisted while the crowd of students grew larger. There was occasional teasing in the corridors after class between teachers and students. One could usually tell in seconds whether or not it was for real, the best sign being whether the student talked back. Sometimes mock arguments and name-calling broke the tension, and the teacher and student emerged good friends. A quick look at Sadao pressed up against the lockers outside the social studies classroom with his teacher edging toward him was enough to tell anyone that this was no game.

With their faces inches apart the teacher erupted with the episode of Sadao's complaining about his mispronouncing Fujimitsu. "You didn't like that, huh? You think your name's that special? That it? All these kids in the school, but your name is special, more than any of theirs?" Still the boy didn't speak. The students too were silent. Sadao could feel the locker air slits on his arms and the metal against the back of his head. The moment had come. "And suppose," the teacher leaned down toward him, "that I mispronounced your name altogether and just called you Teddy the Jap?"

Instinctively, Sadao pushed off against the lockers, slamming his palms against the doors. Tightening his lips he struck out and shoved the teacher away from him. His hands hit squarely on the teacher's shoulders. The man tumbled backward but never lost his balance. He could have caught himself sooner, the students would say later, but he made it appear that the blow was stronger than it actually was. He was smiling as he righted himself and looked about at the stunned faces of the students. It was precisely the reaction he had wanted to evoke, but Sadao was not finished. He spread his legs slightly and raised his fists as though openly challenging the man to fight. The teacher continued smiling.

"You chickenshit son of a bitch," Sadao barked at him.

The man stood facing the student. "You just made your second bad mistake, pal. I might have forgotten the first one, but no one here gets away with that. And there are a lot of witnesses. You better consider yourself out of school for a long time, sonny boy. Hitting a teacher and then swearing at him on top of it? You're going to be gone a long time, friend. Talk about mispronouncing your name, there isn't going to be anybody saying your name around here for a long, long time. You might as well empty out your locker right now. I doubt they'll let you stay here the rest of the day."

Sadao stood still, his posture unchanged. The teacher seemed surprised that his words had not convinced the boy he was beaten. The students now were beginning to yell out to Sadao to lay off, that he was already in enough trouble. Everyone knew that suspension would be an automatic penalty. The teacher's provocations would be lost in the description of Sadao's menacing shove and his swearing. Still the boy did not budge, and when he reached behind himself and slipped his hand in his backpocket, the students became quiet, and began withdrawing while the teacher stepped back, his smile gone, his face showing fright. In the next instant, surely the boy would flash a switchblade in the teacher's face. The hall was silent. Everyone watched Sadao.

His face expressionless, Sadao jerked his hand from his pocket and thrust a bright red comb in the teacher's face. Then, with exaggerated casualness, he ran it through his hair, pulled off a few loose strands, replaced it in his pocket, grinned and walked away. The students were dazzled, the teacher infuriated.

Three days later after long discussions and arguments involving the faculty counsel, student honor committee, and Mr. and Mrs. Fujimitsu, Sadao was suspended for the remaining three months of the school year. Whether or not the administration would allow him to make up the lost time or force him to repeat the entire year would be decided by the end of the summer. Sadao's side of the story was taken into consideration, as were the reports of thirteen students who had witnessed the episode. Every student saw the teacher as having provoked the incident and felt Sadao's talking in class did not warrant the teacher's remonstration. The teacher sent an official apology to Mr. and Mrs. Fujimitsu who, throughout the deliberation, could not decide what hurt them more, the teacher's use of the word "Jap," or their son's actions.

In the end, no amount of argument overturned the suspension. No student, the principal said, can ever be excused for pushing a teacher or swearing at him. If order is to be maintained, nobody can be allowed to go unpunished after doing what Sadao did. Through an official letter from the principal, the Fujimitsus were advised that the teacher had been warned that no such episode was to occur again and that an investigation of his record, dating back twenty-one years, would be undertaken. The matter was not unfinished, the letter said. Each side would have to pay a price. Sadao was assured of being readmitted in the fall, assuming good behavior during the months of the suspension. The letter concluded with a personal apology for what had happened and an assurance that everyone was proud to have other Fujimitsu children attending the school. What happened with Sadao would not prejudice the treatment of these other children.

If Rynosue Fujimitsu was angry at the school, he never communicated it to anyone outside his family. The night the letter arrived he had a talk with his son. Neither father nor son told me what had been said, only that they had conversed in Japanese. Mr. Fujimitsu let me read the letter. When I had finished, he took it from my hand in the same gentle manner Sadao would have shown, folded it neatly along its creases and placed it in the top drawer of his desk. Never once did he comment to me about the misspellings of his last name, which occurred twice. The only information that Sadao confessed to me about the conversation with his father involved the misspellings. Never, his father told him, was he to mention these mistakes to anyone. They were unforgivable errors, his father had said, but they would have to be overlooked.

The teacher's provocation of Sadao was enough to convince the boy's relatives and friends of his innocence. Mike Tajima, especially, was hurt by the suspension. He told Sadao that had it been him, he would have pulled a real knife from his pocket and stuck it in the teacher's face. He threw his hand forward as he spoke, the gesture frightening Sadao. "You just be a good boy and they'll take you back," he said. "Maybe they'll fire the teacher. Maybe we'll get the teacher in our way." Mike Tajima's tone was serious, but Sadao knew that the man's gentleness would prevent him from retaliating.

On several occasions Sadao brought this point up to me. "Was it good," he wondered, "for people to be so kind they don't fight back? I'll have to decide that," Sadao said almost to himself. "Someday, I'll have to see where I stand on that one."

Whatever else Mike Tajima and Sadao talked about, Mike's love for the boy never wavered. Shortly after the suspension, Sadao entered his basement studio to find out that it had been redecorated. Working at night, Mike had built additional shelves and dragged in two antique trunks for Sadao to use. On the front door he added the word "PATIENCE" alongside the word "LUCK." Sadao was uplifted by the remodeled studio. For several weeks he set about to paint and make light constructions, plans for which he had long ago drawn up. Within the month he had a job working as a delivery boy for Tamura Akira, whom the neighborhood children called Tommy. Tamura's cleaning and tailoring shop, besides being the best of its kind around, was also the meeting place for many older people. Every afternoon one could find several old men sitting in the back of the store, warming themselves in the winter by a potbellied stove while Tamura attended to business as if he were alone. Occasionally, he would throw in a word to their conversations but usually he barely paid attention.

Both Tamura Akira and his cousin Yoko Okamoto, with whom he shared ownership of the store, could see unhappiness in Sadao's eyes and manner. The instant he came to them seeking work they knew he was troubled. Sadao wasted little time telling them of the fight at school and the suspension. Tamura was outraged by the teacher's action, but Yoko Okamoto felt that Sadao's response had been unwise. What did he think the teacher would do? she asked Sadao, shaking her head the same way Mr. Fujimitsu had done when he heard the story for the first time. Still, both Tamura and Yoko saw the need for Sadao to work, and since their other delivery boy had just quit, the job belonged to Sadao. Yoko promptly suggested a salary. Tamura Akira argued it was too low but eventually gave in. Sadao hardly cared. The final offer was more than enough. He even refused additional money Tamura promised to pay him secretly.

"I agreed to take what you and Yoko offered," Sadao said.

"You're a good man," Tamura told him. "The school did wrong. You will prove that to them."

Between his art work and the new job Sadao kept busy. But no amount of activity could hide his sadness. "I should be in school," he told me shortly after the suspension. "I feel terrible watching my brothers and sisters go to school. I can even sleep late if I want to, 'cause Yoko says I don't have to be there before ten. But I see all the kids going to school. That's where I should be. The school should have thrown the teacher out too, but they never do that. You see the way it works. What it comes down to really is words. That's what you learn from things like that. The school has to decide what's worse, him pushing me or me pushing him. I'll bet if I didn't say anything they might have let it go. Even pushing him didn't have to matter that much. He can call me what he called me, but I can't swear at him. It's just words. It's like you're in an office, like the principal has, and you got these two lists of words up there on the wall, you know what I mean? One list is words you can use, the other list is words you can't use. What they're saying is swear words are worse than calling my family Japs. It's communication. They don't know how bad that word is, 'cause if anybody said it to them they wouldn't even hear it. They'd probably look around to see where the Japanese guy was. But like, when some kid is called a nigger by a teacher . . ."

"Are they?" I interrupted him.

"*Are* they? You kidding me? They're called nigger all the time. One of the assistant principals is black, and he can't even stop the teachers from calling the kids that. But what I was saying is that when they call some kid a nigger, I always feel like they could be calling me that too. It's like they were really talking to me. But we don't have anything to call them back. So we swear behind their backs. This time I decided the guy had to know how it feels. When I saw my words didn't hurt him as much as his words hurt me, I decided I'd do something to scare him. So I did that thing with the comb. Guys do that all the time to each other. Kids watching knew I wasn't going to do anything, but I saw that teacher get scared. I don't care what he told anybody. He got my message. He was scared!"

While Sadao's words at first might have made me think he was reasserting his pride or even planning revenge, it was sadness, a feeling of having been betrayed and perhaps hopelessness as well that I heard. The suspension had crushed him. Long ago inured to the problems of discrimination and racial hatreds, the exclusion from school depressed him, cut into his energies and even affected the loveliness of his motions. It was not the lack of justice that saddened him—although it angered him—as much as it was the reality of being deprived of the chance to learn with the other students. He felt he was missing out; that there were things one heard and said at a particular time in one's life, and that if one missed that time, one missed those communications and lessons. And there was no way to make up the losses.

One May afternoon Sadao and I met at Tamura Akira's shop. It was a hot day, and for once no one but Tamura was there. Sweat poured off his face as he packed clothes in thin cellophane sacks. Sadao entered the store from the rear obviously hot but grinning from ear to ear.

"Boy, have I got news for you," he said, grabbing my arm and practically dragging me out of the store.

"What's going on?" I asked.

"I got a brain storm. You think I'm pretty good doing art things? Like the constructions out of wood, and the lamps?"

"I think you're terrific."

"You think I do all right with those kids in the day-care center, teaching them to read English and stuff?" Obviously setting me up for something, Sadao was sounding like a little boy.

"You still doing that?" I hadn't inquired about the day-care center since the suspension.

"Sure. Why should I stop? But you think I'm a good teacher though, right?"

"I think you're great," I again answered dutifully.

"Really, man?" He looked at me seriously. My response had been honest, but he needed more support.

"I think you're a terrific teacher, Sadao," I said slowly. "You know how much I admire your work with those younger kids."

"All right. Here's one for you. You think I could start a school?"

"A real . . ."

"A real school. Students, classes, books, the whole thing."

"By yourself?"

"You don't think I can, do you?" He began looking sad.

"I didn't say that."

"You think it though, don't you?"

"No, I don't! What are you planning?"

Passing over any judgments I might have had, Sadao began his explanation. "I'm going to start a school for kids who are out of school. Kids like me. Young ones, my age, maybe some older ones too. I was thinking there are all these kids around here not going to school for one reason or another. Mainly they don't speak English well enough. So, we'll teach them. I got three people in with me already."

"Mike Tajima, I'll bet is one," I said happily.

"Mike's going to teach. So is Tamura and my mother. We'll specialize in communication and creating."

"Fantastic," I blurted out.

"You really like it?"

"I love it."

"We're starting right away. Kids can learn anything they want. Anyone who wants to come can come, either as a teacher or a student. I thought maybe we could write letters to the schools and tell them how the kids were doing if they wanted to get back in or maybe start school for the first time. Some of the kids around here, you know, have never been to school. This will be the first time."

"And where will you do it?" I wondered, recalling the stories of free school and alternative school administrators killing themselves trying to find buildings, warehouses, lofts.

"Guess!"

"Property of Sadao Fujimitsu. Luck. Patience," I answered with a smile.

Sadao grinned and nodded. "Good, eh?"

"Better than good. Tremendous. When do you open for business? Can I visit?"

"One week from today."

"What took you so long?" I kidded him with a perfectly straight face.

He was taken aback, before he recognized the humor in my question. Then he laughed. "Just waiting for your approval." He pulled out his red comb and ran it through his hair. Noticing that I was observing him he suddenly got serious. "I guess I better get a new comb, huh?"

"You're nuts," I kidded.

Sadao nodded cheerfully. "You better believe I'm nuts. I'm the new principal. From now on *I* do the suspending. Anybody gets out of line *I'm* the guy who throws them out."

"How about saying if anyone gets *in* line you'll *think* about throwing them out?"

"All right," he agreed. "No suspensions. No red combs either." Sadao jumped off the curb and ran down the block to the nearest sewer basin. "So long red comb," he shouted toward the sky. He kissed the comb and waved it in my direction. I waved back weakly. Sadao looked at the comb, then knelt down and dropped it in the sewer. He waited, listening for it to hit bottom. By this time I had caught up to him. Didn't make a sound," he said with surprise. "I didn't hear it hit. How do you like that? Anybody down there?" he yelled into the sewer. He put his ear to the street. "Nothing," he muttered under his breath. Then he dropped his voice trying to create the effect of an echo chamber. "Hey, who dropped this comb down here? This is the teacher's lounge. No students' combs are allowed down here. Don't bother us. That's better," he said to me. "I knew it'd get there sooner or later."

Within days Sadao's school had accepted its first pupils. Five children began daily lessons in English and drawing, Sadao teaching both subjects. Mrs. Fujimitsu helped care for the younger children. By the end of June twenty-eight children were coming every day to attend language and art classes. Mike Tajima appeared every morning. Proudly, he had assumed responsibility for cleaning the basement studio that served as the single classroom. He found small chairs in a school warehouse somewhere, painted them bright colors, and put them in the studio. He also located several large canvas cloths, which he laid on the floor so the children could paint without fear of spilling.

Sadao taught two classes of English in the morning and one large art class for children ages five through ten in the afternoon. He bought himself a professional ledger book in which he kept records of the students' progress. In time he had written detailed histories of each of his students. With all this work, he still found time to assist in the day-care center and work parttime for Tamura Akira and Yoko Okamoto. All the while his little Communication and Creating School was gaining a reputation in the neighborhood, and he was becoming a local celebrity. Students from his old school offered to help him, and he accepted them all. To say the least, his July report of the school's development was impressive:

"We've got a faculty now of nine people," he announced. "That means our teacher student ratio is always good. When we teach English, I make sure some of the other kids are sitting near the children so we can be sure everybody's learning what they're supposed to. We got some money for books from parents. I may start a library. Mike has a whole lot of shelves ready for us. I'll get a librarian. You know Susan Ito?" I shook my head. "Well, anyway, she'll be the librarian. It's a tough job, 'cause she has to make a list of the books that come in and then make a catalog. I think we'll ask each family to give us five books. We could have two hundred books in less than a week's time.

"My plan is to have someone at the school every minute of every day. A real school should be open all the time. There's always got to be someone there too, 'cause sometimes people just want to sit and talk.

School isn't always learning, learning, learning. Some kids just want to talk, so, we got to have a place for them. And some kids want to come in at night, you know, so they can paint and do work. We'll have a place for them too. *Real* schools think they can get you to do creative things from, like, 9:20 to 10:10 on Tuesdays and Fridays. But no one works that way. Sometimes when you want to build something you just have to sit there. Maybe you don't do anything for a month. You just sit there, you know, hour after hour. Nothing happens. Nothing ever happens when you want to be creative, and you got a teacher looking at your paper every five minutes. I want kids to come and paint when they want to and make things when they want to. That's the way creating works. Learning English for those little kids is different though. They have to be taught. You have to use a lot of discipline with them. You go over the same things, the same words over and over again. The next day they forget it, so, like, you're starting from the beginning every day. But that's all right, 'cause nobody's grading them, nobody's scaring them. It's not creative work, but they got to do it.

"Then once or twice a week I meet with my staff. We talk about what the kids are learning and criticize each other's teaching. That gets a little hairy once in a while. It's hard to judge your friends, but we decided we have to do it to keep us from getting lazy. Some of the older kids think they should be paid. I told them no. They put up a good fight but I didn't let them win. If education isn't free we haven't got a good thing. If kids want to pay, they should go to private schools. Everybody knows private schools are better than public schools. That's what I told them. And anyway, we're a whole lot better right now than most of the public schools around here. You'd have to admit that. Nobody gets suspended. Once you get in, you stay in!"

Sadao's enthusiasm was without bounds. At night in bed he schemed new programs and procedures for Communication and Creating. By the middle of August he had initiated one of these. He expanded the school to include dropouts from regular schools. Communication and Creating was becoming a legitimate alternative community school under the leadership of a fifteen-year-old boy suspended from his own regular school. Visitors were arriving every day to inspect the enterprise. Sadao hosted workers, elderly people, young people from the neighborhood as though they were represen- tatives from the government or the Department of Education. One day a journalist called the Fujimitsus promising to write a story on the school. Sadao almost exploded with excitement. He spent four afternoons preparing the studio, the children, and his staff, but the journalist never came. Sadao was profoundly disappointed, but no one could have known it by the way he continued his work.

By the end of the summer, Communication and Creating was operating from eight in the morning until ten at night, six days a week. One could also find people painting, building, reading or just conversing on Sundays too, for as Sadao had said, a school should be a place for the entire neighborhood. Every day Mrs. Fujimitsu arranged a bowl of fresh flowers at the entrance to the studio. She took great pride in this gesture, and Sadao awarded her a special medal for her help. He made the medal himself out of plaster. On the front he painted a woman's face and on the back he wrote with green ink: AWARD TO MRS. LINDA FUJIMITSU—COMMUNICATION AND CREATING.

The medal was awarded at a party attended by more than fifty people. Mike Tajima gave a speech thanking everybody for making his building famous. He concluded by promising to donate one-half of a month's rent on the upstairs apartments to the remodeling of the school. Sadao flushed with excitement when Mike announced that all construction plans had to be cleared by the school's first and only principal, Sadao Yoshi Fujimitsu.

"You know what I thought when he said that," Sadao told me later, "I said to myself, Fujimitsu, you've arrived. You have really made it. That little idea is an industry now. I mean, I really felt good. One of the teachers from my school came over to see us last week too. She thought it was amazing. She said I should keep doing this. She said she'd teach here if we wanted her to. But Mike, he's really nice too. Everybody's nice. You know we got eleven dropout kids now. Five of them were on drugs last year. That's why they quit. They quit before they were thrown out. They come every night to paint and build. Two of the guys are building a motorcycle and teaching the little kids how to fix motorcycles and stuff like that. And another guy they said was *selling* drugs at school, he comes here every Tuesday and Wednesday night to teach people how to make radios from those kits they sell, you know. We got a letter from his parents thanking us for what we've done for him. They said we straightened him out, whatever that means, and that he's going back to school because of us."

"Who's us, Sadao?" I asked him.

Sadao looked away shyly. "Our staff, I mean. Kids who teach here, work here."

"It means you too," I said.

"Yeah, me too," he replied modestly.

"I think it's terrific. So terrific I got you a present."

"Yeah?" He was genuinely curious to know what I had bought. "What you got?"

"This!" I gave him an envelope with a red comb in it. He was very pleased. Immediately he took the small black comb he had used all these months and snapped it in two pieces. "You mean I'm all right, huh?"

"That's not exactly why I gave you the comb. But you're better than all right, my friend. You're an extraordinary young educator."

"You want to know what this comb makes me think of?"

"The fight with the teacher?"

"Yeah, partly that, but more even. No one here calls me Fudge Pie. They don't even call me Teddy. Everybody here is called the name they want to be called. That's one of the first things we do. When a kid comes to the school we ask him what name he wants to be called. We don't keep official records, only the little things I write about them and who we're supposed to call in case we need their parents. If you want to communicate with somebody, you have to call them by their real name, what they want to be called by, even if you have to spend a year learning how to say it."

While his point was stated with assuredness, Sadao's mind clearly was elsewhere. He kept looking past me as though expecting someone to come through the door. The glancing about was not a typical gesture for Sadao, who took the art of communicating so seriously. His eyes always met mine in conversation, often so intensely that it was I who would turn away with discomfort.

"You waiting for somebody?" I asked.

Sadao shrugged and looked down. Behind him I heard the noise of squealing children. They had just completed painting a mural that obviously had tickled them. "Just once I'd like that teacher to come here so he could see I'm not a bad guy. Every once in a while I think about him. I usually get angry all over again at what he said, but then I wish he'd come here and see what we've done. Maybe he might apologize for his part in it. I would if he would. But even if he didn't say anything about it, maybe he'd go away thinking we're people and not Japs. That's why I want him to come. He hasn't done anything special since that time. They never threw *him* out of the school. I found out. Nothing ever happened to him. He's the same, but I've done a lot. I've worked and done a lot of thinking and did all this too." Sadao pointed behind himself toward the door of the school. "I've changed. I grew but he just got older. I feel sorry for the guy, but I'm still angry at him."

"But you'd like him to come here still." How difficult could it be, I wondered, to get the teacher to visit Communication and Creating? I could invite him here myself. I made a gesture to Sadao as if to say, we can settle this problem in no time. Knowing exactly what I had in mind, he held his hand up to keep me from speaking.

"Don't you bring him here," he ordered. "If he wants to come, he's got to come on his own. It's only five blocks from the school. If he wants to come he'll come. We'll just see what kind of a man he really is."

"But maybe he hasn't heard about your school," I pleaded weakly. "Maybe he's been away all summer."

"He knows about it," Sadao said sharply and turned around and went inside with the other children.

Sadao's hope did not come true. The teacher remained at the school but never visited Communication and Creating, although several other teachers did.

The day before the high school opened in September, Sadao met with the principal, accompanied by his parents. Because of his good behavior and the school he had created, the administration had decided to allow Sadao to be readmitted. Mr. and Mrs. Fujimitsu were very pleased. They didn't even seem to mind that their son's entire sophomore year might have to be repeated. Sadao was disappointed, but his spirits were buoyed by the possibility of making up the spring semester's work during the year and the following summer. Even Sadao's return to school, though, was overshadowed by two events in sudden succession.

That night a friend called Mrs. Fujimitsu to tell of the sudden illness of Mike Tajima. Alone in his apartment he had suffered a stroke. It was several hours before anyone discovered him and took him to the hospital. The right side of his body was paralyzed, and the doctors could not say yet whether he would recover. Mike Tajima's condition shocked Sadao. Communication and Creating, he kept repeating, was really Mike's school. No one else would have given free space and helped as much as Mike had. Families in the building were also saddened by the news, although many of them had believed Mike to be a miserly landlord interested only in making money. Everyone was surprised that he lived as cheaply as he did. The man who discovered him described his apartment as a hovel and said there was no food there. As it turned out, Mike Tajima had been giving a great deal of money to people and to charities, keeping almost nothing for himself.

Before the week's end still another event occurred. Sadao returned from school on a Friday afternoon pleased that his program probably would allow him to make up the months he had lost during the suspension and to rejoin his friends. Outside his apartment building a small group of children who normally would be at work in the studio had gathered. When Sadao asked what they were doing in the street they told him to go inside. He quickly descended the stairs to discover the studio destroyed. The door was off its hinges, books lay on the floor, shelves had been ripped off the wall, most of the constructions and lamps were wrecked.

Sadao's heart stopped. He could not believe what he saw. He closed his eyes tightly, then opened them praying it had been a dream. For a moment he stood in rubble unable to move, unable to think of anyone to call. His father was at work, his mother out, Mike Tajima in the hospital. Finally he sat down where he was and remained there the rest of the afternoon.

Mrs. Fujimitsu found her son in the demolished studio. The police, she said, had learned that one of the neighborhood gangs, a group of high school boys who had been breaking car windows and smashing street lights, might have been meeting at the studio. One night the police kept watch on the building. When they saw some older boys come out of the basement, they decided they had located the gang's headquarters. Actually the boys they had seen had been in the studio repairing a radio for the children.

But where, Sadao wondered incredulously, could the police have gotten the idea that a gang was meeting in his school? A police sergeant, his mother answered, explained that someone at the high school had heard that the studio was "a meeting place for all kinds of kids."

Sadao resolved never to rebuild his school or return to the day-care center. He would, however, keep his job with Tamura Akira and Yoko Okamoto. "I've done all the communicating and creating I'm going to do in my life," he would tell me months later. "If they want that kind of thing again they'll have to get someone else to do it. First I'm a Jap, then I'm a hood. So, let them all be happy about what they did. They aren't going to get me again for anything!"

At school, Sadao's work stays at the same fine level as before, but several of his most admiring teachers worry about a new toughness they have observed in him and a brittle quietness. There is also talk of his running around with a group of boys he would never have acknowledged a year ago. I, too, have sensed a change in him. The grace and eloquence remain—they always will—but the constant manner that characterized him seems less pronounced now, as though it had been replaced by something. We remain friends, but our friendship is not as it used to be. He knows this too, but it is clear that he has no intention of wanting to be close as we once were. "You don't have to keep coming around the neighborhood on my account," he told me recently.

"That's not why I come here," I said, letting him hear my own toughness.

"Okay. I just thought I'd tell you that. I didn't want you to think there was any payoff for you hanging around with me."

"I don't look for payoffs, Sadao," I told him firmly.

"Okay, okay, man" he responded impatiently. "I'm just telling you, that's all. If you're looking for some great story, go find someone else, that's all.

"I'll call you," I said to him when we parted. "One of these afternoons real soon. Maybe we can go someplace." I was afraid to suggest an art museum.

"You want to call me," he said casually, "call me. It's your show. Suit yourself."

"I'll suit myself. I'll call you," I repeated.

"Like I said, man, it's your show."

2.

Special Children, Special Needs

We can never remind teachers too often that all children are special and require special attention. Parents know this well but cannot always act on it. Teachers and administrators know it too, but rarely can they act on it. Most schools are too large, and the demands made on school personnel too great to allow them to teach each child with the care that child needs and for the length of time each human interaction requires. Most children learn quickly that special concern will not be shown them at school. They learn too, usually, that it is not a matter of their personality or talent that results in infrequent contacts with teachers; it is merely that the system of school precludes constant and intense human contact.

What about the children who are really special—who are blind or deaf or retarded or cannot walk or talk properly. Their presence in a classroom distracts the teachers even more from attending to the special needs of the others. Yet surely they must not be shut off from all that schools have to offer. Too many people forget that handicapped children are children, that there are other things in their lives, in their minds and hearts, besides what the world labels as their handicap.

The majority of states have statutes in their public education laws that exempt handicapped children from the right to an education. With all the laws, recent legislation, and funding programs, hundreds of thousands of children are not being educated in public schools. They are turned away because their local school has no special education facility, no special teachers, no special classrooms for the handicapped. In some instances, public schools quote the statute of noncompliance and deny their responsibility to educate handicapped children. In other instances, handicapped children are openly discriminated against. Or perhaps a school will assume the responsibility for educating handicapped children, but in so doing will segregate them to such an extent that their families will be compelled to take the children out of school.

Without public school assistance many families turn to publicly funded state institutions where the conditions are so bad the family cannot in confidence enroll their child. This leaves private institutions as the only viable option for educating the handicapped. Here the problem is exhorbitant costs and few openings for students, with the result that hundreds of thousands of handicapped children receive no formal education at all. They stay home, watched over by their parents or caretakers, and in their lack of educational development, they begin to give the impression of inherent uneducability. The circle closes. We begin to believe that the mentally retarded or handicapped children— even the child who for some reason does not speak English well enough—is not worth educating.

Just such an attitude was challenged in 1972 in the case of *Pennsylvania Association for Retarded Children (PARC)* v. *Commonwealth of Pennsylvania,* which upheld the right of mentally retarded children to an education. Soon after the *PARC* decision, the case of *Mills* v. *D.C. Board of Education* broadened even further the rights of children with special needs to an education. Prompted by these legal precedents, state officials located over 7400 children throughout the United States who had been excluded from school on the grounds of their mental retardation. In 1971 the government's Bureau of Education, a division of the Department of Health, Education, and Welfare, had found that only 45 percent of America's handicapped children were being served in public schools and institutions. As thorough as HEW's survey may have been, the information on excluded handicapped children remains wholly inadequate. No good surveys have been done, no good guidelines for surveying laid down. One would think it an easy task to locate and count these children, but apparently it is not.

For one reason, schools do not want to undertake such surveys. Staffs are already overworked, and the government is not offering sufficient help. Besides, who wants to find children whom one has little interest in educating. There is another problem: Many parents remain ignorant of the special facilities schools now are obliged to offer, and so they remain quiet and hide the existence of their handicapped son or daughter. Some parents, moreover, are unaware of the facts relating to their child's handicap. They believe the labels they hear used and stand convinced of the uneducability of their own children. And some parents, only naturally, are ashamed. Thus, with

Title I funds available for special education facilities in public schools, Americans have only the barest notion of how many handicapped children there are, where they are, who they are.

What little information we do have is saddening to say the least. The Children's Defense Fund reports the following findings: In 1972 Sumpter County, South Carolina, estimated that there were over 1700 handicapped children in their school district, but less than 300 of these children were being served. Richland County, South Carolina, in the same year estimated almost 6000 handicapped children in their district, with less than 2000 being served. In Montgomery, Alabama, less than 25 percent of the school district's estimate of over 8300 handicapped children were being served in the public schools. As depressing as these figures are, we again must recall that they derive from school districts' own surveys. Quite likely, the number of handicapped children excluded from school is even greater. Lastly, many so-called special education classes are inferior, little more than babysitting sessions. The paucity of special education teachers, furthermore, does not help the situation.

If mentally handicapped children pose a problem for schools, then so too do non-English-speaking children. Both groups of children are seen as different and ultimately inferior. And if teachers and administrators turn away from helping these special children, many so-called normal English-speaking children laugh at their "unusual" comrades.

There are some 4 million non-English-speaking children in America, the large majority of whom are not enrolled in bilingual-bicultural programs. From a survey conducted by the government's Office of Child's Research (OCR), we learn that in 353 school districts with more than 1000 American-born minority students, 10 percent of these students are enrolled in bilingual education courses. There are 90 school districts each with 4000 American-born minority children receiving no bilingual instruction whatsoever. It is clear, moreover, that the OCR survey underestimates the problem.

In the 1972-1973 survey conducted by the Children's Defense Fund, over 10 percent of Mexican American children were out of school forty-five days or more. About 8 percent of Portuguese and Puerto Rican children were not enrolled. We noted in the introduction that in one Massachusetts Census tract, more than 73 percent of Portuguese sixteen- and seventeen-year-olds were out of school, and that in one Denver Census tract, 42 percent of sixteen- and seventeen-year-old Mexican Americans were not enrolled in school. The authors of

Children Out of School in America write: "This is a result of inadequate language programs and supportive services, of racially and culturally biased attitudes and practices, and general insensitivity on the part of many school officials to the needs of these children."

The picture of non-English-speaking children is the same in all regions of the country. In almost all the districts surveyed by the Children's Defense Fund, large numbers of non-English-speaking children are either not enrolled in special programs or not enrolled in school at all. In many cases the Defense Fund findings are particularly tragic. In New Bedford, Massachusetts, in 1973-1974, 80 percent of the students in non-English-speaking districts did not receive a high school diploma. In Cambridge, Massachusetts, in 1973, only about 35 percent of the children who needed language assistance were receiving it.

In the District of Columbia, the Defense Fund located two itinerant English as a Second Language (ESL) teachers. Also in the District in 1973-1974, there were 260 guidance counselors, according to Nathaniel Hill, Supervisory Director of Guidance and Counseling, but not one of the counselors spoke Spanish. Springfield, Massachusetts received Title I funds to establish an elaborate social and psychological unit consisting of twenty counselors. Not one of these people spoke Spanish. Some districts reported that Puerto Rican children needed no special language assistance, since they are already citizens of the United States. Some districts had bilingual classes running without a single non-English-speaking student in them. Some districts established ESL classes but housed them in buildings blocks away from the school. Predictably, one-third of the students eventually quit school for good. Some districts established ESL classes in regular school buildings, but the students enrolled in them were attending class a total of fifty minutes each day. In one school-district-based survey, Haitians were considered to be Spanish-speaking, and so their children were assigned to Spanish-English bilingual classes. In another district, Portuguese families were categorized as Spanish-speaking, and their children met a similar educational fate. One hates to think about the destiny of a non-English-speaking handicapped child in this country.

Importantly, all of these events happen in the shadow of Section 601 of the Civil Rights Act of 1964, which bans discrimination "on the grounds of race, color, or national origin." A memorandum to school districts from the Office of HEW had only insignificant effect. Schools continue to openly neglect and segregate non-English-speaking children and assign them to the lowest academic level classes on the grounds that they are ignorant and uneducable. The children are seen literally as a subspecies. One only can assume that the government puts little pressure on school systems to correct this impression.

If one examines closely what happens to physically handicapped and national minority students, one realizes that it is not always the lack of facilities that keeps these children out of school, as much as it is a school's reaction to children who appear different. A child who walks with crutches, wears thick glasses, or stammers is seen as out of the ordinary, so too is a pregnant girl. There is nothing special in the way of educational materials a pregnant girl requires. Yet, despite laws that prohibit schools from excluding pregnant girls—for example, the precedent set by the 1971 *Ordway* v. *Hargraves* case in Massachusetts—thousands of pregnant girls are out of school. To this day there are no standard policies relating to pregnancy for school districts. Moreover, if the girl gets married, her chances of returning to school are not appreciably increased.

The statistics on schoolgirl pregnancy may surprise some people. According to Cyril Busbee, South Carolina State Superintendent of Education, one out of every ten school-age girls is a mother. One-sixth of this group is less than sixteen years old. About 60 percent of pregnant girls get married; about 15 percent give up their babies for adoption. "Pregnancy," Busbee said, "is the major known cause of school dropouts among girls in the United States." It is, but one should linger on the word "dropout," for a close investigation of these cases reveals that pregnant girls are pushed out of school more often than they drop out of their own free will. The school's message to them: School activities will upset their physical and mental state; their pregnancy is a bad influence on other girls; classroom order cannot be maintained if pregnant girls are present; and the school cannot possibly offer day-care, much less prenatal-care, facilities. Not only is the pregnant girl viewed as weak, she is seen as creating chaos and corrupting the values of her classmates.

In 1972-1973, 62 percent of the female dropouts in Montgomery, Alabama, reported pregnancy as the reason for their dropping out. In the same year 1300 girls in South Carolina listed marriage or pregnancy as the reason they dropped out. In a 1974 Georgia survey eighteen schoolboards had a written policy that pregnant girls were required to withdraw from school. In one Kentucky county, pregnant girls out of school were allowed one hour a week of homebound education. Throughout the country pregnant girls are being turned away from school and sent to all sorts of so-called alternative learning centers. While some of these centers may satisfy the educational needs of a particular student, many of them deny entrance to pregnant girls. In Prestonsburg, Kentucky, for example, the Children's Defense Fund discovered a local rule prohibiting married students from enrolling in the Neighborhood Youth Corps In-School Program, this according to information from the director of that program.

In the remainder of this chapter, we examine life studies of children and their families, who have experienced exclusion from school on the basis of English-language deficiencies, physical illness, mental retardation, and pregnancy. There is a fifth study as well. It is a study of a young man with an acceptable school record, excluded from school when it was learned that he was a nocturnal bedwetter. The outrageous character of this particular exclusion case does not in itself merit its being recounted here. It is included because it confirms the unlawful discrimination against children merely on the basis of their being, somehow, different—imperfect. The case of this boy demonstrates, moreover, that the peculiar qualities that make a child special and evoke in school authorities reactions that result in the child quitting school, need not be perceivable. Merely knowing that a girl is pregnant, just being aware that a boy has epilepsy or wets his bed at night—although the episodes never occur at school—may be sufficient barriers to enrollment.

As long as she could remember, Caroline Ritchie wanted four children. As a girl she made a solemn promise to have four like her mother and grandmother. Ideally, there would be two boys and two girls, but it didn't matter as long as they were healthy. Every woman probably thinks about that, she used to say, especially when something went wrong with a child in her family. Although no one ever confirmed it, it was said that her mother's mother gave birth to a strange sort of child. One look at the infant, and everyone knew it wouldn't grow up to be normal. Its head, the story went, was enormous, its nose was flat, and its eyes were set so far apart it was difficult to imagine the poor thing being able to focus them. No one in the family, however, knew the fate of the child. Indeed, to this day, Caroline Ritchie is not certain of the child's sex, nor how long it lived. She asked her mother many times, but answers were not forthcoming. "They had ways of dealing with those kinds of children then," her mother replied. "And besides, why's a little girl like you so interested in things like that? You can't grow up thinking about the bad. Look at life and be thankful about what's good, what grows up healthy, like you."

For years Caroline Ritchie was unable to forget the stories of that strange baby. She dreamed about it, and imagined doctors placing the child in a hospital somewhere, or her grandmother locking the baby in a secret attic room of an old house. Perhaps the baby froze to death, or perhaps it grew up to be normal. Maybe it was still alive. Maybe animals, not understanding it was a human being, ate it. Again and again she went to her mother and inquired about the child. It was clear from her mother's evasiveness that such a child had been born, but her mother gave no information. "Think about the good, Caroline," she always said. "The bad is for the devil and gossips."

As the years passed, the mystery of the strange baby assumed less importance for Caroline. By the time she married at nineteen, she had forgotten about it entirely. Not even her first pregnancy a year later caused the memories to return. Like many expectant mothers, she experienced a variety of worries before the birth of her baby, but nothing triggered the return of the stories that had preoccupied her as a child.

Charles Ritchie, Jr., was born on the day Caroline's doctor had predicted months before. He weighed a little over seven pounds and was in perfect health. He even had a full head of hair.

Maintaining her wish to have four children and buoyed by the easiness of the delivery, Caroline waited barely a year before getting pregnant again. Charles Ritchie protested that his salary as a steel worker wasn't rising fast enough to support two children, but Caroline insisted. A second son, Ronald, was born twenty months after Charlie, Jr. A healthy, robust baby, his early visitors just knew he was destined to become a football player. Charles, Sr., was especially pleased by the arrival of his second son. A small raise at his plant helped in paying doctor and hospital bills.

In the course of two years everyone in the family recognized that Charles and Caroline were moving up. They moved to a larger apartment, and with some of their money and space problems solved, few were surprised to learn that Caroline was pregnant again. Charles joked that he was aiming for a basketball team; Caroline said she would not quit until they had a girl.

For no apparent reason, Caroline wondered more about this baby than the others. The doctor answered her questions and tried to assure her that he could find nothing wrong, but the last two months of pregnancy were filled with fits of anxiety, dreams of terror and death, and a loss of appetite.

Nevertheless, a third son, Howard Riley, was born without problems, and with the shortest labor Caroline had yet experienced. A trifle over six pounds, bald, red-faced, Howard cried so loudly it made the nurses laugh.

Caroline's relief from the anxiety was almost as exhilarating as the birth itself. She thanked God, her doctor, her mother, her grandmother (even though the woman was dead), her three sons, and of course Charles, who already was talking of a fourth.

This time Charles was the first to suggest having another baby. "I may not get the basketball team," he told the doctor, "but one more and I'll have my infield." Everyone razzed Charles. "Ready to have another, eh?" "Why not?" was his answer. Caroline merely demurred, "He's the boss."

Apparently, the talk of a fourth child was serious, for a year and a half later Caroline was again pregnant. The boys were doing well, and Charles's job was holding up. They'd been lucky so far, they agreed, so why not try to stretch the luck one last time. But this was definitely it. No more children, even if the fourth wasn't a girl. It made Caroline sad to think that at twenty-eight, her child-bearing years would be over, but the thought that she would be growing up with her children pleased her.

The fantasies of the strange child in her family history returned. The fright was nowhere near as intense as it once had been, but the same old rumblings were present, giving Caroline nightmares and making her anxious and overtired.

At last it was time for the delivery. As in her previous deliveries she was put to sleep without pain. She awoke hearing the voices of her husband and doctor. A nurse was handing her a daughter, Gloria Myra. Charles was smiling down at her. Caroline again had the feeling, as she always did, of wanting to leap off the operating table.

"You lost your infield," she would say to Charles.

"It's better like this," he would answer. "Anyway, infields are cheap to get. It's outfields you pay a helluva lot for."

They would talk easily the rest of the afternoon and evening. The next morning, after she had eaten her breakfast with Charles lounging at the end of the bed, he would tell her what the doctor had told him. "There was a chance," Charles said, doing his best to repeat the doctor's words, that Gloria had sustained a certain amount of brain damage. There was a good chance that no noticeable damage had occurred. In fact, the doctor said it might have been unnecessary for him even to mention the possibility. But there was also the chance that some things could go wrong. That development wouldn't be totally normal.

"Like what?" Caroline asked frantically, feeling herself wanting to cry out.

"Like speech, or learning. I don't know for sure. We have to wait. That's what he said. It could also be nothing. No one knows. The worst it could be is special schools, that's all. It's not the end of the world."

Caroline lay her head on the pillow. Her eyes were dry, and she felt as though her body had gone dead. "It's worse than the end of the world, my friend," she whispered. "It's the end of the world for that baby. If you aren't normal, there's no sense being alive. Everybody knows that. Little things are different, even missing a finger or a toe. But when your brain isn't working you're a vegetable. No matter what anybody says, you're either a human being or a vegetable, and she's a vegetable!"

"It's not true," Charles tried to comfort her.

"Don't lie to me. You should have told me yesterday."

"The doctor said wait 'til today."

"I gave birth to a sick child, a vegetable."

"You didn't. We don't know the extent of anything."

"Don't lie," she whispered. "I know. I'm the mother of that child." She wanted to say strange child.

"I'm the baby's father," Charles said gently.

"It's not the same. It's never the same. Your child doesn't have a chance. You better face it, we're three for four. Oh, God," she moaned. "What do you tell people? And what in the world do you tell the child? You're really fine, baby, it's that all the other kids in your class are weird. It's not that you're dumb, it's that your brothers are smarter.

"Caroline," he said at last, "if you want to see it as the end of the world, go ahead. I don't happen to see it that way. We don't have the faintest idea what's going to be with her. There's a lot of kids with problems, you don't even know there's anything wrong with them. Jesus, the kid isn't a day old, and you've already got it figured out what she'll be like in twenty years!

"Anybody can be a mother when their baby is healthy. Anybody can be good with kids like ours, the boys I mean. Real mothers are made when things like this happen. I made my peace with it the second I knew. There was no decision. You're going to have to do the same."

There was nothing in Gloria's first year that signaled trouble. Early in the second year Caroline noticed that the child's utterances seemed peculiar. Certain reactions, too, were slow, although these characteristics could be attributed to the fact that Gloria merely was different than her brothers. By the end of two years, though, it was evident that the child's language and learning capabilities were, in Caroline's word, "flawed." There was a serious problem, but still the Ritchies had to wait until the child's development unfolded more. It was Caroline's wish that they visit medical specialists throughout the city, but Charles kept reminding her that their income allowed for only infrequent consultations. There was little to learn at this time anyway, he argued.

"There's plenty to learn," Caroline protested. "But if we don't have the money, we don't have the money."

Gloria turned four in the same year that Caroline reached thirty-two. The child seemed happy and had become the special prize of her brothers, though her speech was slow, and often incomprehensible. Ronald acted as an interpreter, but occasionally he, too, became exasperated when he could not make out his sister's words. Charles remained constant. The growing seriousness of his daughter's condition distressed him, but he hid any fright or sadness he might have felt. At work he told his friends there was something wrong with his daughter, but that things were going better. Anticipating the financial strain of a special school for Gloria, he began investigating various placement possibilities. But without state support, he could afford nothing but a regular public school.

Unable to settle on an appropriate course of action, Gloria was withheld from school until she was five, when she entered the same neighborhood kindergarten attended by her brothers. The principal met with the Ritchies and assured them that several teachers were sufficiently trained to deal with Gloria. There had been other students like her in the past. Pleased that the school accepted Gloria so readily, the Ritchies hardly fretted over Gloria's discomfort in the first weeks of kindergarten. Gradually, she felt more at ease until she hardly noticed her mother or father leaving the kindergarten room.

By Christmas, however, it had become obvious that she needed more help than the school could provide. The class had been unusually large, the principal told Caroline and Charles. Perhaps everyone had underestimated how handicapped the child actually was. Charles merely listened to the principal, a woman in her late fifties with silver hair and little puffs of skin under her eyes. Caroline sensed his anger.

As for herself, she heard the word handicapped as though someone had shot her in the face. She had never used the word to describe Gloria, and yet she could not disagree with the principal. Nor could she fault the woman's tone. The word had come out sounding objective, scientific. The child was handicapped.

Inevitably, the Ritchies withdrew Gloria from school. The child seemed unperturbed by the action. Caroline, waiting for some response of disappointment, fell into a sadness on recognizing Gloria's inability to demonstrate normal emotional responses. Until that point, she and Charles had concentrated on the muscular and cognitive weaknesses. Aware, naturally, of the sweep of children's emotions, they simply had not witnessed their daughter in enough situations to consider the possibility that the damage to Gloria's brain had affected her feelings. There was just too much to look for in the child.

Once again, Caroline tried to ward off the feelings of hopelessness and eternal optimism and settle on some realistic middle ground. It was like Charles had said, one had to be perfectly honest about the child's chances. That meant recognizing progress as it came. And it did come, although with deathly slowness.

The kindergarten experience represented the first tangible failure. Believing that school would reveal the problems that would always haunt Gloria's life, Caroline had bypassed the opportunity to send the child to a neighborhood nursery, despite the urging of its director. "Many mothers," this woman had offered, "are afraid of reterdation and brain damage. But more than anything they're afraid to watch their child in school. As long as they keep the child at home nobody's around to make comparisons. You can always say the child's behind her older brothers and sisters because she's younger. Parents even lie. They tell themselves, maybe she's all right after all. Maybe I just forgot how long it took my other children to talk and read. But once they get the child in school and pit her up against so-called normal boys and girls they realize where they stand. That's one of our biggest jobs," she had said, "convincing parents they haven't failed. I stay with them when they watch their child play and I practically feel them ready to fall over. If they could just see their child at that moment they'd realize she doesn't have the slightest feeling about being inferior or retarded or handicapped. But the parents do. In that moment, they cannot see their child. They can't see anything. Nursery school is partly for them too."

Caroline had trusted the director but never enrolled Gloria in the school. Thus, nursery school was forfeited, and a year later the kindergarten experience, too, had ended. Caroline could justify the absence of schooling by claiming she had more time to strengthen Gloria's confidence. Charles, however, had noticed Caroline's embarrassment about Gloria. He accused her of being relieved that the kindergarten rejected the child. Caroline denied it but knew that he was right. She had reached the point of wishing that Gloria would stay small so people would think she was too young for school.

When it came time for first grade, Caroline again registered Gloria in kindergarten. This time she was openly refused admission. It was the school's understanding, she was told, that all of this had been settled. The Ritchies would have to try elsewhere. Upset by the rejection, Caroline tried to get Gloria admitted into other kindergartens near their home. Everyone wondered why she had waited so long. One school said no on the grounds that they were not in the Ritchies home district. Another said there was space for Gloria but withdrew their invitation when they saw the child was handicapped. The school's assistant principal strongly admonished Caroline: "That should have been the first thing you told us. We don't have facilities for children like that. Send her to the Cromwell School; they're set up for children like your daughter."

Now accusing Caroline of intentionally keeping Gloria out of school, Charles took charge of his daughter's application to the Cromwell School. As it was already late September, the school said no. The most they could offer was a tentative acceptance for the following year. Charles returned home disconsolate. The only remaining options were two private institutions that charged exhorbitant tuition fees. When he heard what his share would be even after partial state support, he never bothered to call either school. Gloria, presumably, would remain home another year and face the possibility of never attending any school.

Hiding his last hope from his wife, Charles Ritchie called several state mental hospitals, all of which advertised facilities for retarded and brain-damaged children. With a friend he visited one of them and found it to be far more pleasant than he had envisioned. His wife was ill, he told the woman who showed them around. He was merely inspecting the place. But when he inquired about costs, she announced a figure of over six thousand dollars a year. He had been misadvised; the school was not public. He felt ashamed, and the woman was annoyed that he had taken her time. Going home Charles found himself weeping for the first time in his adult life.

A week later he visited another hospital. This time he had called in advance and inquired about annual expenses. Although the drive was almost an hour, Charles felt optimistic. The grounds of the hospital were especially lovely on a sunny October afternoon. The offices seemed not unlike the public schools Charles and his friend had attended. Both joked about "being with the loonies" and hoped they wouldn't be visiting the wards. When offered to be shown around, Charles insisted on seeing only the school for special children. It seemed as though they walked forever. The friend, whom Charles had introduced as his brother, laughingly complained of the size of the campus. "It's like college," Charles told him. "Like these big colleges with famous football teams."

After passing through locked corridors, high-walled courtyards, and rooms that looked like dormitories, they reached the classroom. Charles was horrified. The room was huge, poorly lit, and empty of color. Many of the children were sick in a way he had never seen. Some sat in the middle of the room on little chairs wearing helmets and rocking. Others sat on the floor perfectly still. Some paced aimlessly back and forth, and one boy kept running into a padded wall. Everything was shabby, and an ugly odor filled the room. Charles politely retired to the men's room where he vomited on the floor. He refrained from washing his face and rinsing out his mouth for fear of touching the sink faucets. He left the hospital without seeing the schoolroom again.

There was no need to visit the last hospital on his list, his friends had said, it was worse than this one. Nor did he tell Caroline of these excursions. One of the hospital administrators called Caroline at home, however, although he had given hospital administrators his office telephone number. Caroline pretended to know about Charles's interest in the hospital and reiterated his decision not to send Gloria there, but at the conclusion of the call she wept. When she asked Charles why he had never told her about the hospitals, he said that he had thought of them as possibilities, that was all. She had made the right decision, he said. Hospitals weren't for them unless they had a million dollars.

As was now his practice every day, Charles drank with friends after work before going home. Caroline never mentioned this new behavior of his, but it was obvious to everyone in the family. Charles, of course, was more than merely aware of the frequency of his drinking. The experiences involving Gloria had begun to eat away at him, as he said, and caused him to feel hopeless, not only about her, but about his own life apart from her as well. Night after night he lay awake, unable to endure the anxiety and restlessness that he felt he had to keep from his family. Playing with the boys, once a source of pleasure, had become a burden, especially at night when they fought his orders to go to bed. And just watching Gloria tediously working on a puzzle made him feel angry and useless. Within a short time she would turn seven. In all these years, she had attended school less than four months, and nothing lay ahead in the future.

"I sit there night after night and watch her," he said to me, a friend of two years, on the eve of Gloria's birthday. "Night after night. I dread the weekends when I have to be home with the four of them all day. Of course I drink. People at work, everyone in my family knows that. Anybody can see why. I told my wife the day that child was born I'd made peace with her condition, no matter how bad it was going to be. The doctor could have said that afternoon that by the time she was four she'd be a vegetable, a hulk, you know, lying in the middle of the living room, and I would have said that's all right with me. It's not that, it really isn't, and she isn't that bad off. Next to the children I saw that day in the hospital, I tell you she's normal. You can't believe how terrible those kids out there look, especially with no one taking care of them. There are degrees to this thing, you know.

"But you can live with a retarded, brain-damaged, handicapped child, whatever you want to call them. You can live with it plenty easy. Hell, *they* live with it; they cope with it better than anybody else around here. Believe me, I see it. The youngest boy is terrific; the other two are, you know, a little this a little that. They don't want to tell you how they're feeling. Every once in a while they'll say, 'Daddy, is she ever going to be all right?' Something like that. 'Is she ever going to get better? Will she be like that when she grows up too?' They have the courage to ask the questions their parents would like to ask. So I can live with it, or maybe I should say I can live with her. But when something like this school business happens, it's not only the child you think about, or live with. That's only part of the situation. *You're* the situation. You and your wife. If you're strong there's no sick child in the world can make you see yourself any other way. They can't budge you. You just stand pat, make your peace with it and stick it out as long as it takes. The rest of your life if needs be. The birth of my sons, see, were like a sign that everything was pretty good. Marriage was good, my job was good. But Gloria coming into the world—and we wanted her, don't get me wrong about that—she was a sign that things weren't going to be so good anymore.

"That child came, seven years ago tomorrow afternoon, something like four o'clock. Now, you have a new child, what are you thinking about in the hospital? You're thinking how's your wife, how's the child, and how you're going to pay the bills? God forbid, something could happen to your wife or your child, hell, you could be faced wih burying both of them, but you'd have to come up with the money, Somebody hits me with a couple thousand dollars in bills, where do I go? And let's say you can come up with this money, like I couldn't come up with the money for a private school for Gloria. But let's say I could pay the bill, what do I do next? Where do I get the money for the next bill, you know what I mean? Here comes a retarded, handicapped kid into my home, here she is, day after day. Every day now is a reminder that *I'm* the one who's handicapped. That's what I was never able to face straight on before her. She's the one everybody can see is having problems, but I know that *I'm* the one who's less well off than most of the men in this world.

"The days I visited those hospitals were what settled everything for me. When I compare those two schools they had, the one that was perfect and the other one where I saw those kids banging their heads against the walls, that was the true picture. Those rooms told me that if you don't have the money for a good situation you end up putting your kid in a room like that one, which I swear wasn't set up good enough for an animal. So now I walk around wondering what to do with my kid. When someone asks me I tell them Gloria goes to a fine school, and she's happy, you know, and we're real pleased. I lie. I lie, and I drink.

"I'm drinking because we've denied the problem with that child from the beginning. Both Caroline and me, we both had in mind that you can pretend either that there's nothing wrong with the child, or that whatever is wrong will go away. Like that, you know what I mean? Magic. One day everything turns up fine. So here we are with a seven-year-old kid who's handicapped. I hate the word; I hate what it means financially to us, but you can't pretend things are different. Children pretend, adults deny, and somewhere in between those two is the man who drinks!"

Caroline Ritchie would not say she had denied "the problem," although she admits to wishing she could run away from it. She berates her husband for his weakness, which she claims the drinking represents, but she appreciates his sense of failure and hopelessness. The seven years with Gloria have had their moments of happiness, but confusion, distrust and a desire to settle the child's future dominate Caroline's thoughts. She wants to love the child and protect her, but she wants to blame her too, as illogical as she knows that is.

"In the beginning," she said a week after Gloria's seventh birthday, "I suppose I reacted foolishly. I confess to wishing the baby had been born dead. I know how horrible that sounds, but it's true. I told Charles, but he refused to listen. I created quite a storm about it in the hospital. The nurses hated me for saying it. They must have thought I was deranged. It was strange, because even though I was saying it, I really didn't mean for it to happen. It was like I felt I had to let people think I was separated from the baby; not only was she not a part of me anymore, she had never been a part of me. Like, I couldn't be the mother of a retarded child, otherwise there was something wrong with me too. If I pretended to kill Gloria, I could kill myself, or the part of me that made her what she was. I wasn't proud of saying all those things, but I honestly felt them.

"Then there was the part about the strange child, my sweet little leftover from childhood. It was like the reason I held onto that memory was because it was being arranged that *I* would have the strange baby. It doesn't make sense, I told myself that a million times, but when I began remembering the stories from when I was a kid and I was pregnant with Howard, I knew I was in for it.

"But the fourth child brought out too many old superstitions. First, was the feeling that I'd had three and things had gone too well. Then I decided that the strange child memories and my old desire to have four children was going to produce the bad magic. I kept telling myself after Gloria was born that I should have known four was the bad number. But it wasn't always bad; I mean, there are lots of times when it's been good. Like there are times when I still have the wish that Gloria had never been born, but then there are times when I'm glad she was born, retarded I mean. We'll do something together, like I took her to the circus about a year ago. Just the two of us went. I remember at intermission we went to buy food, and I felt great, like I had discovered a whole new source of energy in myself. I was really happy being with her, she was six then, and everybody who looked at us could see there was something wrong. But it didn't bother me. In fact, I was glad she was like that. It was like I was saying to them, I'm this girl's mother and you don't know that I have three healthy boys at home. You think she's all I have and that's exactly what I want you to think. I'm proud of this child. You think she's handicapped, but I think she's special. I wouldn't trade her for all the healthy children in the world. I wouldn't even trade her for a healthy her. This is the way she was born, this is the way everybody meant for her to be, and that's the way she is.

"Those feelings don't last that long. Sometimes while I'm having them, I'll imagine making Gloria famous. You know the ads with a movie star and a crippled child? I imagine that Gloria could do that. Or sometimes I'll pretend that I've started this crusade for brain-damaged children, and people begin to hear about me and vote me the Mother of the Year. The highs and the lows. One minute I want her dead, the next minute I'm using her to become famous. Maybe both these feelings are part of the same thing. Maybe they're signs that I was shocked, disappointed. But you can't blame anybody, and you don't particularly like telling people what's happened. You tell your husband, 'It's you and me, Buster, how do you like what we just made? Pretty super, isn't she? Pretty terrific!' Then I have this peculiar feeling that I don't want my husband to know.

"I suppose the worst people are the ones in school. The second they see Gloria they're already figuring out the situation. I always think they're blaming me for what's happened or because of the way I'm treating her. I always want to tell them, I'm really a good mother. You should see me when I'm alone with her. Why don't you blame *her*? She makes my life hard too, you know. It isn't just the other way around. She makes it damn difficult for me, even when I'm not with her. I don't put her out of my head like you teachers can do with the students. You go home in the afternoon and forget the children, but we're with them all the time. I don't care what they say, I always think they're disapproving of me some way. Like Gloria could be much better off than she is. I could have taken Gloria to the doctor more often, but every time I go, he always says there's nothing I could have done any different. The big things they advise cost a lot of money, so we do what we can. But I don't see where these school people have the right to judge us the way they do, or at least the way I imagine they do. They don't take her. They've got all the excuses in the world why she doesn't fit in. Everywhere I go they have all the best advice for me, but nobody says, sure we'll take her and help her to learn. So I'd have to say I'm doing better than any of them.

"I think about having more children. Maybe trying just once more. We won't, but I play with the idea. I'd like to know whether it would happen again. I know that statistics say I'd probably have a normal baby, but we'll never find out. I used to have a fantasy that Charles and I would have a baby. Nobody would know that I was pregnant. We'd go away where nobody knew us. Not even my mother would hear about it. Then the baby would be born, and it would be a girl, and we would name it Gloria, naturally. Then we'd wait a few years and come back and show everybody our *real* daughter Gloria. I don't know what we'd do with a seven-year-old girl so nobody would see us with two daughters, but we'd think of something. Maybe we'd put her in a hospital somewhere, and let the state take care of her, like you see all those people with psychotic children doing. They don't want their children so they deposit them in these horrible places and tell the people they'll come back and pick their children up when they're cured, but everybody knows they'll never come back. They're leaving the kids there for good. Nobody wants those children. It's like leaving garbage cans out in the street on Sunday night. The man comes in the morning and takes them away, and you never have to worry again, unless somebody finds the children and wonders how come you *accidentally* put them in a garbage can.

"I'll tell you something. I don't have to hide the fact that I was crushed by this. I've gotten over it. I'm a good mother. I get help, but when I'm working at it I do a good job. That's bragging, but it's true. I got over the first shock. You never forget about a handicapped child's situation, but you live with it until it only bothers you at certain times. At night sometimes, when I'm alone it gets bad. Or sometimes when we go out with the children, and I'll see a large family pile out of a station wagon I'll find myself watching, waiting for the handicapped one to get out. There has to be a handicapped kid in there. A family can't produce so many good-looking, healthy children.

"Anyway, most of the time I've got everything under control. By the time Gloria was three, we had established a routine with her, and the kind of relationship that a lot of mothers would have been happy to have with their daughters. You have four children and a husband—I have to say that what with all these men walking out on their families and leaving children behind, handicapped ones, too—and an apartment that's way too small, and not enough money, you have a tough job. I don't say the toughest job; lots of people have it harder than I do, but a tough job. But I had it licked. You know what set me back? The schools. I had always counted on them. I assumed when we took Gloria to get her registered there would be no more problems. That would be the end of our day troubles. I didn't want anyone to take her away from us. I assumed that the day routine would be set, and she'd start learning the same things her brothers had learned in kindergarten.

"I even waited. I didn't send her to nursery school, thinking it would be easier to have her home. I thought a child like her is especially sensitive, and I didn't want her to feel people were shipping her off somewhere so they didn't have to be with her. But school lasted a few months and fell apart. Actually, they kept her out. It's almost like they suspended her. They could have kept her, but they didn't want to. They said they didn't have the proper facilities. That's a lot of bunk if you ask me. If you want somebody you take them, if you don't you

"There's a funny connection, you know, between all these things. I go up and down with Gloria. I always have. Sometimes I feel everything's going to be fine, but sometimes I'm ready to quit. I read all the books on retardation and brain-damaged children, technical books along with the magazine articles on parents like us. I know there are experts all over, especially in cities. But it's like everything else. If Gloria were in good hands I'd feel optimistic. It's like when the man comes to fix your stove. You know it's going to cost something, but the moment he comes you begin to feel better. Just him coming makes you feel better. I'd feel the same way if we could get Gloria placed somewhere. God, anywhere. It's like right now, nothing's being done. Doctors can't do anything, schools have all kinds of excuses why they can't take her, so you feel it inside. You get angry, of course, but mostly what you feel is that you're a failure. You're the person who broke the stove, and the stove's still broken. Gloria is still handicapped and she's not getting better spending all this time with me. She's being loved, but she's not making progress. Our whole family's not making progress.

"I suppose what gets me more than anything is what she thinks about. You can tell she understands a lot. I've read books on what handicapped children pick up. Some of the experts say they understand a lot; some say they don't get as much as the parents think they do. We're careful about what we say in front of her. I mean, we don't talk about her condition to her face. We even try not to talk to the boys about it, because they might tell her. But once I'd like to know, does she really understand how she is. If you asked her, do you think you're like other kids, would she know? That's another reason she has to be in school. Someone has to accept her or she'll never know anything, not only about the world, but about herself. And also, I won't think I'm doing my best until she's in the right place.

"I always tell myself that none of this with school would have happened if we were rich. But maybe that's not true. Maybe that's what brings people together. Rich or poor or like us, in between somewhere, we can all share this thing. It makes us alike, at least nobody is better than us. Then again, the rich find places for their children, and here we are having every school say no. So we're doubly worse off. We have a problem with a child, and the school excludes us. It's like we're lepers that people are afraid to let come near them.

"My child deserves a lot more than that. So do my husband and I. We deserve a lot more. We have a right to have that child in school and that's just the beginning. I won't bring up the we-pay-taxes-too argument, but we have a right by token of living where we live. Our child has a right too, although some people seem to think she doesn't. I wish they'd penalize me and not her. They're adding to her handicap, you know. They'll make it worse for her. People can carry on by themselves for a little while, but then they need the society to help them the rest of the way. This child needs even more help than most children, and all they're doing is pulling away from her. And we're running after anybody who'll help. It's so absurd it's almost laughable. It really is. I wonder why we don't laugh. Gloria would laugh if we started laughing. She laughs a lot."

Bennie Marcellino is twelve, although he looks much younger. He has blue-black hair, and eyes that are almost as dark. His relatives jokingly call him "Valentino" after the famous actor, and insist that it is his fate to become a great movie star, but they worry about him too. Since he was a baby he has suffered from epilepsy, an illness that was not properly diagnosed until his third year. Then the seizures became so severe, that no one in the Marcellino family or any of their friends could convince his mother that the attacks were not serious.

Now, as a twelve-year-old, Bennie has received some medical treatment, and the medicine he is supposed to take daily, like dilantin, has reduced the frequency of his seizures. The problem, however, is that the Marcellino family, a mother and nine children—Mr. Marcellino died of a heart attack three months before Bennie was born—find that the monthly welfare check is wholly inadequate; occasionally they are forced to let Bennie's medicine run out. He has had several seizures in recent years, but when the last one occurred in school the principal decided it would be impossible for the boy to remain in his regular classes. School officials blamed Bennie for not taking his medicine, and his mother for not providing it, but more than anything the sight of his eyeballs rolled back in his head, the gagging sounds, the foaming saliva coming from his mouth, and the heavy falls onto the floor or desk, followed by convulsions obliged them to isolate him from the other children.

He was suspended for a week for medical reasons, but when his mother took him back to the school the principal refused him re-entrance because she could not guarantee that the seizures would not recur. Marianne Marcellino argued with him, begged him even to let the boy return to his regular homeroom. She would help him at night with his schoolwork, she promised, but there simply was no place to send him during the day if the school would not accept him. Her husband was dead, she told the principal, and all her other children were in school, or working, or married. Benedetto was the last.

During the discussion I sat next to Bennie. At last the three of us were waiting for the principal's response.

"Get the boy a tutor then. We'll find you someone," Mrs. Marcellino was told. But no one was sent to the Marcellino home. After two weeks of waiting, a school official telephoned Mrs. Marcellino to say that a special class was being arranged for children just like Bennie. It would be for three hours a day. I was visiting the Marcellinos when the call came.

"You mean everyone in the class has epilepsy?" Mrs. Marcellino was more than suspicious for she had heard about these special classes for the handicapped. Retarded children, someone had warned her once, are thrown in with blind and deaf children and children who cannot walk or talk, and children with strange and serious illnesses, illnesses that will shorten their lives. "Why is it only three hours a day?" she asked. "How come all the other children go all day and these children go for so short a time? Wouldn't you think they would go for a longer time?"

It was very difficult to teach these children, she was told. It puts an extra strain on the teachers. Regular teachers can't do the work; they need teachers with special training, and they are not always available. Besides, as a mother of one of these children, the person on the other end said, she ought to know how hard the work is.

"But when he takes his medicine he's just like any other child. You can't tell them apart. He's not blind or deaf or mentally retarded. Every doctor who's seen him says there's nothing wrong with the part of his brain that you learn with. Epileptic children can have normal lives like you or me. There's no way you can tell that they're any different from anybody else." She looked at me and shook her head angrily.

"Take it or leave it," the person replied.

Later that afternoon Mrs. Marcellino proposed the idea of the handicapped class to Bennie. Immediately, his face lost its expression. He refused to go. In fact, he now refused to go to any school at all. The idea of being with sick children upset him deeply. Even if they would let him back in his regular school, he couldn't return because of what everyone would say.

"They call me dumbhead behind my back," he told his mother, ignoring my presence and trying hard to hold back his tears. "Everybody looks at me like any minute I'm going to be sick. They don't want to walk near me or sit next to me. The only time anyone plays with me is when a teacher makes them. I hear what the teachers say too. I hear. 'Don't worry, he won't have one of those things of his.' I'm not going back there. Not now, not never! No one can make me either. And I'm not going to that hospital class . . ."

"Handicapped class," his mother corrected him gently.

"It's a hospital class! They should be in a hospital."

"Don't you talk that way, Benedetto. Those children are trying harder than you are right this minute. They go there, even for three hours, and I'll bet some of them don't like it either."

"Let 'em go. I'm not going anywhere near there. The school wants me to go there 'cause they think I'm a freak. I'm done with school. Been going there long enough," he sulked. "Learned all I'm going to learn anyway. I'll work for Claudio's old man."

Mrs. Marcellino had grown angry with her son. "You're twelve years old," she shouted at him. "What do you know that you're suddenly finished with school? You know that you'll do? You'll work two days for that Abruzzi miser and then you'll stop doing that too. Who do you think needs a twelve-year-old child who quit school? Who you going to work for when that's over? You'll be finished in six months. I give you six months, that's all!"

"I don't care. All I know is that I'm not going back to school. I'm going to work. You don't need to stay here with me. That's all you're worried about anyway. You don't care where I go just so long as you don't have to stay home."

"You shut your mouth. Who do you think you're talking to? You're right I ain't staying here. Who do you think makes the money around here if I don't go out?"

"The welfare check," her son answered bitterly.

"Welfare check wouldn't feed a cat. *I'm* the one who feeds us. With these hands, my friend. You talk like you were someone important. What do you know about working and earning money and raising children? Tell me what you know."

"I know that I ain't going to school." Bennie's eyes were red with tears, but he never wiped them.

"Don't go then. See if I give a damn. Stay here. Work. Go out. I don't care anymore what happens to you." She marched out of the room and slammed the door.

"Ain't you going to tell me to take my medicine?" Bennie muttered when she had gone. "Ain't you going to worry that I might get sick?" Finally, he looked at me, as if he wanted me to side with him against his mother. I said nothing. Bennie just stood there waiting.

Suddenly the door flew open, and Mrs. Marcellino stepped into the room. She flung Bennie's windbreaker at him and started to close the door. "Tell your friend," she said to me, "that whether he's in school or not doesn't matter no more. But as long as he's decided to stay in this house, then he'll have to look after himself like everybody else who lives here. I ain't picking up for no child, especially one his age. Especially one who's *supposed* to be in school!" She never looked at Bennie, but when she stopped speaking I could see that she was hoping he would say something to her, something that might at least sound hopeful.

"Bennie's going to think things through again," I said quietly, hoping to lessen the tension. I looked at the boy. "I really think he is."

"Ain't thinking nothing through," Bennie said flatly. "Thought it all through once and that was enough. None of this happened to either one of you. No regular school, no hospital school."

"Tom, will you tell that boy to stop calling it a hospital school. It's not a hospital school!" she shouted at her son.

"Is too," he grumbled. "It's for sick kids. And I ain't no sick kid." Suppressing sobs, he was barely able to speak these few words.

"I agree," I blurted out.

"Nobody called you sick," Mrs. Marcellino said, coming all the way into the room. Her voice was suddenly soft and kindly. "Nobody called any of those other children sick either."

"They're sick. I ain't going there with them."

"Benedetto," his mother started, "you afraid to go to school? Regular school I mean?"

"No."

"You are too. You're afraid to go to that school." Her voice sounded excited. "I think that's what it is. You're afraid to go back there."

I looked at Bennie to see whether he would admit to feeling fear. His mouth was tightly closed. He held onto his jacket and looked back and forth between his mother and me.

"I'm a bad mother, Benedetto," Mrs. Marcellino was saying, walking slowly towards her son so as not to frighten him. "Your mother, you know that, she's a real dummy." Bennie didn't move. "A dummy," she laughed. "I didn't want to hear you. All I wanted to hear was my own anger. That's all. Your mother's a dummy. Here, spank me." She grabbed his hand. "Come on. One big spank right here." She patted her behind. Bennie glanced at me with embarrassment and began to grin. "Go on. Go on. I was wrong. When you're wrong you get it. I was wrong. I get the spanking."

Bennie looked into his mother's eyes and smiled broadly. He stood perfectly still in the corner of the room. Then suddenly he dropped the jacket and whacked his mother. "That's my boy," she shouted out. She embraced him, both of them crying and smiling. "That's my last child. That's my last child who won't let me down, or his father too, huh?" She held him by the shoulders at arm's length and stared at him. Bennie shook his head. "Go to school? Huh?"

"Which one?" he asked quietly.

"No, no, no. Don't ask which one. Just say, yes, Mama, I'll go to school." Bennie remained silent. "Come on, Benedetto, say it for me now. Yes, Mama . . ."

"Yes, Mama," the boy repeated.

"I will go to school."

"I will go to school."

"Good boy." She pinched his cheek and bent over to kiss him on the top of the head. "Now we can get going with this thing. This boy here," she said to me, "he's been crippled by his school. He's no cripple, they did it to him. But we're not going to take it, are we?" Bennie did not say a word. He just looked down. "They've had their turn; now we have *our* turn. Of course, he doesn't want to go in a hospital class." She winked at her son. "Why the hell should he? He belongs in school with kids just like him. There's nothing wrong with him. One month he's gone from there, isn't that right? How long you been out of school, Benedetto?" Bennie didn't answer her, but his silence did not ruffle her. "About a month, I'd say. And I'd also say they owe you that month. So what we're going to do is either go there and put you right back and make them call the police if they don't want us, or put you in a whole different school. What do you think of *that*?"

At last Bennie smiled up at her. I could see that he was not altogether pleased, but I knew too that the idea of his dropping out of school and hunting around for jobs that he probably could not find, pleased him even less.

"You see the way they got it rigged, Thomasso?" It was Mrs. Marcellino's pet name for me. Bennie enjoyed her making everyone an

Italian. "They got it now so that it says a boy Benedetto's age *has* to be in school. Is that not so?"

"True." I answered her.

"But do they also have a law that says just because a boy isn't *exactly* like everyone else he can't go there?"

"There's no such law." I enunciated my words clearly to let Bennie know I was on his side too.

"Well Tom, it seems to me," Mrs. Marcellino was saying, "that they ain't going to kick anybody out of that school just to make it easy for *them*. Not until they show me that law and tell me I obey it or I go to jail. You want to know something," she said, looking at me, all the while holding tightly to her son, "I *would* go to jail for this. Sure, I got to have him out of the house. But it's not just being out of the house that matters. It's being *in* school. Children have to be in school to learn. If he's not in school he breaks the law and I see a failure looking at me in the mirror. All ten of my children go to school. We get Benedetto his medicine and he goes. He plays sports too, huh?" She looked at her boy. Bennie's enormous eyes were clear and shining. "You play with those kids. Basketball, baseball. No football," she said sternly. He nodded. That warning had been issued many times before. "I'll play ball with you myself," she laughed. "Thomasso, you play ball?"

"Sure."

"You'll play ball with Benedetto. You play with this big man here," she told her son, "you'll have the kids coming to *you*. But I'm not finished." She pointed her finger at me. Bennie and I were still smiling at the thought of our playing ball together with his mother. He seemed embarrassed. "We're going to see how it works out. If Benedetto likes it being back there he stays. If he don't we move him to another school. Thomasso here will find you another school. How's that sound Benedetto?"

"Okay," he whispered.

"One school stinks, we go to another one. Schools are just like fruit anyway. If one feels bad, throw it back and take another. You choke on the bad ones."

For a few moments it seemed as though everything were settled. Mrs. Marcellino was nodding her head triumphantly, I was going through names of people in my mind to call in case Bennie's school continued to refuse him re-entrance. Then Bennie broke the silence.

"What if they don't let me back?" he asked. "I'm still, you know, like before."

Marianne Marcellino was waiting for the question. "Then we do something else. We make war. You know what war is?" She looked at her son who nodded. "Well, that's what we do. We make a little war right here in Boston. Not a big one, but big enough. And you know who starts this war?" she asked her son. "Mr. Thomasso here starts the war." She looked proudly at Bennie, who in turn looked at me incredulously.

"He *does?*"

"He does," Mrs. Marcellino repeated authoritatively. "Generalissimo Thomasso starts the war. In the court. I want to know for sure whether they can keep this boy out of school. If they can, we go somewhere else. If they can't we go to war, with your lawyer and professor friends. Rich people got ways. We got nothing. You'll figure something out."

Uncertain of what to say, I just nodded my head.

"Thomasso starts the war, but none of the Marcellino children get hurt. Before it starts we make sure Benedetto's safe in another school. Huh?"

"I hadn't stopped nodding.

"Okay. That's settled." She pushed back her hair and glanced about the room to see whether there was something she should do now. Bennie was still looking mystified at me.

"Don't look at him like that," Mrs. Marcellino ordered her son. "He'll do it. He'll do it. And pick up your jacket please and hang it in the closet."

Bennie bent over, picked up his windbreaker and walked out of the room.

"You'll try and help us," she said to me when he had gone. "All I want from you is a promise. Can you give it?"

"I promise."

"He admires you like you were his own father, you know. So I had to let him know you'd be with him in this. It's like you'll be going to school with him. You know what I mean?"

"Yes."

"He wouldn't go anywhere alone, but with you doing something for him, he'll go. What I do isn't enough."

"We'll do something."

"You mean with lawyers?"

"Why not?"

"You brought up my welfare check one hour ago, that's why not."

"We'll get lawyers," I assured her. "There's a case here."

"You've been standing here so long, would you like something to drink?" She suddenly sounded old.

"No, thanks, Mrs. Marcellino."

"Can I ask you something?" she put her hands on her hips.

"Of course."

"You want to help Benedetto, don't you?"

"Naturally."

"Then make sure he'll always have medicine. For the rest of his life. You know what's going to happen? Unless we find the perfect school, they'll wait for one of his seizures, and we'll be right back where we were today and last week. I can't keep bringing him back there. I can't do it. Wars, law courts, hospital schools, I'm running out of ideas. I'm running out of energy. He's the last of the nine. The last one. His father never knew him. That makes him very special. You know, I've always believed that the problem he's got might have been put there by God to make sure everyone knew how special he is. I won't let them do it to him again like they did in that school. No special classes. No special treatment. He's not different from anybody. A regular school, a regular class. That's what a special boy needs. Maybe too, Tom, you can find a school where a couple of people might like him. I mean on top of letting him in, they would feel it was important just to like him. He's a lovely boy. You can see that. There's no reason they couldn't like him, on top of, you know, letting him go to school like all the other children."

In the summer of 1965, Maurice Broyard, a cement worker, brought his family from Haiti to the United States. When the Broyards landed in New York, Maurice wore a sign around his neck with his name on it, for he, his wife, and the four children they had brought with them were to be met by someone they did not know. They waited on the dock for eleven hours, before a man came for them in a small station wagon. A friend of a cousin of Mrs. Broyard's, the man drove them from New York to Boston and delivered them at the home of the cousin in Cambridge. Upon completing the trip, the man turned around and drove back to New York. The Broyards could not thank him properly, for he spoke no French and they spoke no English.

The Broyards moved into a three-room apartment that they shared with their relatives. Mrs. Beatrice Lecesse welcomed them warmly, although their presence meant that there were now ten people living in the three rooms.

"We'll get more mattresses," she smiled at them. "We've done it before."

Maurice promised to find work at once and move his family into an apartment of their own. But there was no work. The few construction jobs he could locate in Boston had been filled since early spring, and little hiring went on during the winter. Landscaping, cement work, and yard work were even more difficult to find. Christienne Broyard found a job caring for the children of a Cambridge family who had recently returned from a year in France. They wanted her to speak only French with them. She agreed, laughingly, claiming it was the only language she could speak with anybody.

Beatrice, in the meantime, arranged for the three Broyard children to attend the local school with her own children. The youngest Broyard daughter was too young for school. Phillipe Broyard, ten years old, and his other two sisters would walk to school each day accompanied by their three cousins, the Lecesse children. Money would come in, Beatrice assured a disheartened Maurice, who more and more doubted the move from Haiti. Still, there was little chance of his earning a living there, so the trip to America seemed necessary.

In his first weeks in the United States, Phillipe Broyard stayed close to his cousin Angel. He was learning English words more quickly than anyone in his family, and he believed that by the time school opened in September, he would be able to get by. He had fun during the days exploring the neighborhood, and sleeping in a room with so many children was actually sort of pleasant at first. The children rolled around, giggling and playing while their parents decided that since it was vacation and everything was new to the Broyards, the children should be allowed to have a good time.

A week before school opened, Phillipe suddenly grew sad. He began speaking about his friends in Haiti and the toys he had left behind. He begged his parents to go home or at least send him back. He could stay with his older brother, he told them.

"Nobody's going back to Haiti," his father said. "We make our home, our friends, our money here. Pretty soon you'll be an American."

The words meant nothing to the boy who now was frightened by the prospect of school. His English vocabulary was growing to the point where he could go to a store and purchase simple items. He could not, of course, read, or understand people when they spoke quickly.

"Slow for me," he would tell them. "Slow for me. Haiti. I Haiti."

"Haiti, eh?" they would say, and do a little dance as though to say we know about your island. Phillipe's eyes would glow with excitement and pride.

The night before the opening of school, Phillipe had a dream that he recited for his mother.

He is about to leave Haiti. He stands on the dock ready to board the boat that will take him to America. He looks around for his mother and father, but they are not on the boat. He is only mildly worried although confused, for he thought they would be traveling with him. Then he sees that the President of Haiti is on the boat, standing on a deck above him, so he feels relieved.

As the boat begins to move, he waves to his friends, all of whom have come to say good-bye. Somewhere in the enormous crowd that has assembled on the dock, he spies his mother. Like the others, she is waving a handkerchief. "Where is my father?" he calls to her. She points behind her. He sees his father working with a lot of men. They are building an airport runway next to the dock. His father is so busy he doesn't see that the boat is pulling away.

Soon the people on the shore are barely visible, tiny specks that he can just make out. He walks to the railing on the other side of the boat and sees the shores of America. Again there are people on the dock he can barely make out. They are waiting for the boat to arrive.

Suddenly he hears the passengers yelling and crying. There is a fire in the bottom of the boat, and the captain is ordering everyone to jump into the water. He takes off his shoes very carefully, stuffs them in his pockets, rolls up his pant legs, and jumps over the railing. People everywhere are splashing about. They seem to have friends—only he is alone—but staying afloat is no problem for him.

As the boat begins to sink, he hears the captain calling out on a public address system. "You are between Haiti and America. If you swim the other way you will be in Haiti. You can do whatever you like." Phillipe sees that the two shores are of equal distance from him. He decides to return to Haiti. He swims and swims. Each time he looks up the shoreline is closer and the people on the dock appear larger. He is not out of breath or fatigued. He knows he will make it. He is entirely without fear.

At last he reaches the dock. He climbs up a wooden ladder out of the water, takes the shoes out of his pockets and puts them on, rolls down his cuffs, and walks toward the crowd. Everyone is welcoming him and praising him as a great hero and fine athlete. But they are speaking

English. By mistake he has arrived in America. He awoke from the dream trembling.

For two weeks Phillipe attended the school ten blocks from his home. His English was improving, but whenever teachers called on him he said nothing. Finally, one of his teachers made him see an assistant principal. Believing he had some learning problem or even neurological impairment, she wanted advice. Phillipe went to the assistant principal's office but said nothing the whole time he was there. The principal took out his record and thought of calling his home, but no telephone number was listed. A policeman was ordered to take him to a Cambridge hospital for tests, and Phillipe went, mistakenly believing that the policeman was driving him home.

At the hospital, by coincidence, a nurse assigned to interview him turned out to be Haitian. When she pronounced his name in French, his eyes grew large and he began to speak without stopping. Phillipe explained the problem at school. The nurse cancelled the medical appointment and telephoned the principal who reported that there was nothing in the records about his being French-speaking. Beatrice Lecesse had avoided listing it when she enrolled the boy, for fear that the language problem would mean he could not attend the school. The principal was pleased to learn that the problem was so simple and told the nurse to advise Phillipe that a special program would be arranged for him. He could continue going to school, and his parents would be advised of the program he could enter. He said he would also make arrangements for the boy's two sisters who, because they were younger, were having an easier time in kindergarten and first grade.

The young nurse, Andrea, called on the Broyards to assure them that the school had promised to put their children in a class with French-speaking children from several Cambridge schools. "Pretty soon," she told them, "Phillipe here will be teaching the rest of you English." The family was delighted with the news.

"At last we're in America," Maurice Broyard declared. They celebrated with a bottle of wine and laughed when they saw an Italian label on the bottle.

But for Phillipe the occasion was not altogether happy. For the first time he felt self-conscious about the conditions of the apartment. He could tell that Andrea had been surprised by how poor the family really was. "We're going to move soon," he told her outside as she was about to leave. "My father has this big job he's going to start working on."

There was, of course, no job. In fact, the little bit of money Beatrice had saved up was almost gone, although she never complained. The money brought in from Christienne's job barely paid for the rent and food. In addition, Phillipe's youngest sister was suffering from asthma, and the cost of medicine and a week of hospitalization could not be covered in the welfare regulations set up for Beatrice. Maurice found occasional jobs, but the money they yielded was expended as fast as it was earned.

To make matters worse, an English learning program was not established for Phillipe. In February, six months into the school year, he had still not been placed in any special class. Inquiries brought promises and guarantees, but nothing was settled. On a freezing cold day Phillipe walked forty minutes to the hospital seeking help from Andrea, who had become the family's adviser. He arrived only to learn that Andrea had left Boston to take a job in a hospital in Montreal.

In school Phillipe remained shy, unwilling to try his steadily growing English vocabulary. He still could not read, and at home only French was spoken. A teacher recommended that he watch television and listen to the radio even if it was just the news because the announcers spoke so clearly. Phillipe promised to follow her advice, unable to admit that his family owned neither a radio or a television set. Instead, he sneaked into the movies in downtown Boston through stage doors, telling himself that movies would help his English. Gradually, the movies and downtown adventures grew more interesting than school, and he began cutting afternoon classes. Later on he didn't bother with morning classes either and began being absent for days at a time. Because he had been deemed "unteachable"—some teachers continued to believe he was brain damaged—no one at the school bothered much with him. At first they called on his home to question his absences, but because it meant a special trip, it was inconvenient to keep going to the Broyard's apartment.

Christienne Broyard visited the school twice with her employer, who spoke for her. A French student program was "in the making," she was told, but at the end of the school year Phillipe had not been enrolled in any special class. The year was wasted. His spoken English was now adequate, his English reading and writing skills were nonexistent.

By the following summer Maurice Broyard had gained sufficiently steady employment to lift his sadness and make life financially adequate for his family. But there was still not enough money to allow him to find his own apartment, and, in addition, Beatrice's home had become a station for Haitian immigrants. At times more than twenty-five people lived in the three rooms, babies sleeping in drawers and cartons, the older children sleeping four and five to a bed. Phillipe was hanging around with a group of older boys who, like him, spent a great deal of time out of school. They called him "Haiti," which pleased him.

When school opened in September, Phillipe was administered a series of tests along with an examination to check his perceptual abilities. His reading scores were so low that the school decided to fail him, rather than merely keep him in the same grade. Now eleven, he was assigned to the fourth grade. He refused to accept the class assignment. He was too big, he said, and too old. He wanted to go back to Haiti. Since nobody cared about him anyway, he told his parents, why not let him quit school and get a job. His parents would have none of it. The most important thing, they replied sternly, was to go to school. Anybody living in America who has finished school will be successful, they promised him. Phillipe returned to school.

On the basis of the test scores, the school decided that a special French class was no longer necessary. Phillipe should have no problem doing his work, particularly since he was in the fourth grade. Moreover, if he did well, the school would jump him into the fifth grade. In fact, he did well for almost a month, when gradually his number of absences began to increase. First, as before, he cut school after lunch. Later, it was the whole day. He continued to be the special friend of the older boys he had met the year before, some of whom were becoming involved in minor crimes like shoplifting and handbag-snatching. Phillipe was called upon to work with them. One of their favorite routines was to have him ask a wealthy-looking person for directions. He was perfect for the part, they said, because everyone fell for his accent. While the victim was helping Phillipe, one of the older boys would grab the person's briefcase or purse.

Scared at first, Phillipe quickly began to believe that he and his friends could never be caught. It did indeed seem that they were invincible until one afternoon, after pulling the routine on an elderly woman, he ran right into the arms of a policeman. The woman identified him, and the policeman took him home. No one was at the apartment, and so they waited for two hours. Suddenly, Phillipe dashed out of the police car and ran away. The policeman left but returned that night to tell the story of the robbery to the Broyards, who were frightened by their son's disappearance. The police would do nothing this once, they were told, but if it happened again the boy would be prosecuted and so would all the adults in the apartment, for housing illegal immigrants. Some of the families who had stayed with

Beatrice Lecesse had come without passports, and while the police knew about them, they were willing to remain blind to it all if the children stayed in school.

Phillipe returned the next day, having slept at one of the older boy's houses. His father whipped him with a belt and dragged him to school. He told his son what the policeman had said. Phillipe was frightened and ashamed. He promised never to go with those boys again. He hadn't realized, he said, that his parents could get into trouble. He blamed his problems on the school, saying that he could not do most of the things the other kids could do, and he was afraid they would keep flunking him. His father argued that he was looking for excuses. "There was no reason that a boy his age couldn't be as smart as the babies in his class." The remark hurt Phillipe, but he never said anything else to his father on the subject.

Within a month he was back with his friends, working the old purse-lifting routines and listening to their plans to rob restaurants and bars. In March, a year and a half from the time he arrived in the United States, with his school reports telling of definite progress, he and three boys, all of them fifteen and older, were caught stealing money from a bakery store. The money was found in a paper bag held by Phillipe, since he looked like the most innocent. This time a policeman took the Broyards to the jail where the boys had to stay overnight. Christienne Broyard wept. Her husband felt so ashamed and angry he was barely able to speak. A friend of his from work accompanied them and acted as interpreter. One of the first things the police did was to run a check on the Broyards with the Boston and New York immigration offices. Phillipe hoped he might be sent back to Haiti.

"The only place you're going, Haiti baby," the policeman told him derisively, "is jail. And don't think we don't have 'em for kids your age. We do! Lots of them. Maybe you can learn to speak right while you're there."

The following morning the boys were released in the custody of their parents. Several days later they went to court. The older boys, all of whom had prior police records, were later ordered to a reformatory school. Phillipe, after intervention by a lawyer and a psychologist, was placed on probation. The judge demanded that a special class be found for him. He advised Phillipe that the court was giving him a second chance because of the difficulties of coming to a new country. "I'm being sympathetic in this case," he told the Broyard's lawyer, "because of the boy's age, but don't let me see him in this court again. He's had his chances, foreign or not!"

Within two weeks Phillipe Broyard was placed in a special education class for French-speaking children. In it were students from several Boston communities. Almost at once, his spirits lifted. Just to be able to speak French with children outside his family made him happy. He insisted that his parents speak only English and that they read the newspaper with him for a few minutes every day like his new teacher suggested. He made friends with four Haitian families and discovered that several students in his regular school were also French-speaking.

"The school was bad to do what they did," he said, as his special class went into its sixth month. "They should have taught me English. Not just speaking, but reading and writing too. You can speak a language and not really know it. But they let me in and didn't help me. I was there and I wasn't there at the same time. They never threw me out, but when I was there they didn't care about me. They even thought I didn't speak up in class because there was something wrong with me. With my head. That's what they thought. What they don't know is that lots of children get embarrassed when they can't speak or write like they're supposed to do. They don't know that. What they could have done is let the other kids hear what French sounds like, but they didn't do this either. They can't speak French, and they don't think children have anything to teach.

"They never threw me out of school. They never said you can't come into the school. But there are different ways you can stay away from school. I was ashamed to be there. The teachers never called on me in class, because they knew I couldn't read and they said they had trouble understanding me. But if they had made me speak up I wouldn't have said anything anyway. I was too afraid. So I stayed away. My father knew what I was doing and why I was doing it. He knew I was ashamed. Even the time the police got me and he whipped me, I knew he knew why I did what I did.

"Poor children go to the worst schools. If I went to a good school I never would have cut class. They wouldn't have let me. I wouldn't have wanted to. They could have taken care of me. But this school, they lied. They could have helped me; they just didn't want to. They said it was too hard. So I stopped going. Everybody would do the same thing. They don't really like the children in the schools, especially the ones like me who are different. If you talk funny or look funny or are different, then they don't like you so much. They really want you to leave because you just make extra work for them. And see, if they throw you out of school, then *they* get into trouble with the police because they're not supposed to do that. But if you stop going, then *you* get in trouble with the police and they like that better. I think they'd like me to go back to Haiti so I would never bother them again.

"They once took me to a hospital to see if my brain was all right. They weren't even smart enough to figure out I didn't speak English. I was afraid to speak the words I knew because I knew I had a terrible accent. So they thought there was something wrong with my brain. When I started going there I liked it, even though I was afraid. I thought they liked me too. But when they took me to the hospital I saw what was in their minds for the first time. They're the ones who should go to the hospital, because even though they speak English there's still something wrong with their brain. They need a brain operation, and some medicine to make them nicer."

Phillipe Broyard continues to be somewhat afraid in school, although much of his shyness has diminished. He speaks in class when he is called on, but rarely volunteers to say anything. He and his family continue to believe that not only did the school fail him, they in effect suspended him. They cannot be certain, moreover, that the boy's earlier troubles may not return. Phillipe has said that "life is better," but a doubt that began the moment he and his family left Haiti, a doubt that he believes should have subsided by now, persists. And then there is a dream, which recurs as often as twice a month, that continues to frighten and perplex him:

He is walking into his school on a rainy day, happy to be inside. The school is pleasantly decorated and all the students seem eager for their morning classes to begin. He enters his classroom and carefully chooses a desk in the middle of the room. Children enter the room and soon all the desks are occupied. He is waiting anxiously for his teacher.

Suddenly the door opens, and the school's principal stands before the class. He is very tall and wears a dark brown suit. "Phillipe Broyard," he calls out loudly, "you must stand up." The boy rises slowly, already feeling ashamed. "You do not belong in this classroom. You do not belong in this school. We don't want you here. All the teachers and all the students have told me that they don't want you. You must go home. Right now. Not to your apartment but back to Haiti. You are too poor and not smart enough to be here. Leave your things and go now." The children giggle and call out names as the boy leaves the room.

Always Phillipe awakens from this dream with anxiety, and always he is relieved by the sight of the sleeping children who share his bed, and who, he knows, share so many of his feelings.

It used to be that merely stating that someone was, say, fourteen years of age, was enough to provide a picture of that person. Fourteen meant not a child, not quite an adult, someone on the way to maturity, a freshman or sophomore, presumably, in high school, someone probably just feeling the early feelings of intimacy. Maybe too, someone rebelling from his or her parents, thinking about a career for the first time in realistic terms.

Now, however, as the evolution of our culture has altered the very meaning of time and age, to say that someone is fourteen means very little. At long last, we are beginning to recognize the extraordinary variation in fourteen-year-olds, in fourteen-year-oldness really. There are, to be sure, an enormous number of fourteen-year-old girls and boys safely and not so safely settled in schools. There are also fourteen-year-old girls and boys in reform schools, detention homes, "houses of delinquency," and strangely too, living, according to Census materials, in homes for the aged.

*A*nd then there are some, like Maxine Dolan who, at fourteen, has an eight-month-old son to care for and wants to make certain that there is love shown this boy, and enough money to provide all the things she knows a baby needs. Still, she wants to return to the school that suspended her when they learned she was pregnant, the school that remains unwilling to let her return on the grounds that she committed an egregious sin and now represents a dangerous influence on other girls.

"What do they think I'm going to do in that school, teach everybody how to make babies or something? I'll bet that's what they got in their minds. That I'll come into all their classrooms and interrupt them. 'Hey Teacher. Kids here don't want to learn how to do their mathematics or social studies. They want babies. That's what they want. They're sitting here wanting to make all kinds of little things running around on the floor.' That's what those folks think. I see it in their eyes. They don't need to tell me nothing. They think all us girls don't want anything but just to get pregnant. They think that's all we're doing, making babies. Well, they don't know, 'cause they don't know us. They don't want to know us neither. When we behave they let us stay, but the minute we stop behaving they tell us we got to get out of there.

"Well, I say this: They haven't got any right to throw me out of that school, pregnant or not. I've never seen a rule that says pregnant girls or mothers can't go to school. I don't see any reason in this world why if I can find someone to take care of my son they can stop me from going to school. That's my right. I'm not a bad influence on anybody. Fact is, if you ever talked with my friends, you know, like Gloria, or Sara Jane, or even Margaret, who always says she thinks it's so great to have a kid, they'll tell you, privately I mean, that they're really glad it wasn't them. I can tell that too, just from looking at their eyes. They wouldn't change places with me for all the money in the world. And that's saying something too, 'cause a hundred dollars to their mothers would look all right. So you see how it really is, I'm a *good* influence on those other girls, girls that are supposed to be my friends. Hell, I'm the best influence that school could have. They couldn't find a better influence than me. Anytime one of those girls was thinking she might do something foolish, all those teachers would say is, look at old Dolan, that's how you'll end up if you ain't careful. Just look at Mama Dolan, sitting there rocking her baby, and she's only fourteen years old."

When Maxine learned that she was pregnant, she went first to her friends Gloria Canner and Margaret Reyes, both of them thirteen years old. They discussed the choice between abortion and having the baby, knowing that the child's father would never take any responsibility. In fact, he never visited the hospital and has seen the baby only three or four times, and these by chance. Maxine's mother angrily insisted on an abortion, but her grandmother, sixty-year-old Clarissa Meers, was more sympathetic to the child's situation. She suggested that to begin, the family consult the school. "Perhaps they have ideas on what to do," she said. "Maxine couldn't be the first child to have this happen to her."

A guidance counselor agreed to meet with the three women, Maxine, her mother, and grandmother, but the interview was short and the advice simple: Whatever the girl did it had to be done outside of school. Nobody pregnant could attend classes. After the baby was born or an abortion performed, they could meet again and decide what to do then.

"But why can't this girl go to school like she's supposed to until the last days?" Clarissa Meers demanded to know.

"She just can't," she was told. "That's the policy and nobody's about to change it. You know, Mrs. Meers," the guidance counselor added, "you make it sound like this girl's accident was *our* fault."

"I'm not blaming anybody," Clarissa Meers replied sternly. "I'm only wondering whether there isn't a problem just settling the child's right to go to school. Any school."

"I'm afraid," the guidance counselor said, "that any right she ever had has just gone out the window. You all should have thought about this before." That was the last time any of the three women entered the school. They never bothered to speak with the assistant principals, as they were advised that the school administration would be even less open to discussion than the guidance counselor. Maxine Dolan remains out of school. The time is just about right to make an application for reentrance, but now another problem has arisen: Can she face the humiliation that so many people in her school cause her to feel.

"You take, like that baby actually coming," she said once. "That ain't half as bad as the feeling of being out of school all these months. It's been seventeen months. And don't you think for a minute that I ain't counting them. First there was all that time waiting for the baby, and then I had him, and then I had to take care of him. Or maybe they just thought you can have a baby and leave him somewhere, like on the street, maybe that's what they think, and just go tripping back to school. Well, you can't do that. You have to take care of a baby, love him, 'cause you're all he's got. You could pass him over to your mother, or like in my case, to my grandmother, but that's not why that baby was born. He was born for me. I'm his mama, and there's nothing I'd rather be, but I'm still sorry that they made me leave the school, even if I did make a mistake. My baby would be better off if they let me go back, but all they can think about is that there ain't no mama going to school.

"See, I'm willing to pay the price. I know I should be married. I know this is going to be one horrible mess in the future too. No one needs to tell me that. That's the part I'm living everyday, anybody can see that. But now, I'm going to be two years behind, and that means I got to start my freshman year all over again, right from the beginning, and be going to school with kids two years younger than me. That part scares me a lot. If I tell them I have a baby, they won't want anything to do with me, which they probably won't anyway 'cause I'll be so much older, and if I don't tell them, they'll think I've been flunking in my classes.

"They never should have made me leave that school. They ruined it for me when they did that. They made it so's the only thing I can do is get the worst jobs in the whole society. There's nothing for me to do. They made it happen just this way. Even at fourteen I could be a mother and still go to school, finish high school like most of my friends and then see what might happen. But they ruined it. I don't think it's fair. Their job is teaching, not making all kinds of rules that end up hurting people. School matters a whole lot, you know. You go on to college and you've got it made. You can be almost anything you want. If you just finish high school you're in pretty good shape, even if you have a baby. But who do you suppose wants anything to do with an eighteen-year-old girl who's never finished much more than eighth grade and has a baby and doesn't know anything? What am I supposed to say when they ask me how come I didn't finish school when I was supposed to? What do I tell them? They didn't let me? I wanted to go to school, and they didn't let me? You tell that to anybody and you just know what they'll say: 'Miss Dolan, this here's America. Every child has the right to go to school regardless of race, color, creed, or religion. If you really wanted to go to school when you were fourteen, I'm sure the school in your community would have been glad to take you. You must have done something pretty bad to make them keep you out of there!'

"Well, I'll tell you, Judge." She was speaking to an unseen authority, but it seemed as though she could see the inside of a courtroom. "The only bad thing I did was to tell people I was having a baby and then go ahead and have him. That's the horrible thing, Judge. What I probably should have done is murdered somebody, somebody real old probably 'cause no one misses them, and then I could have gone to jail for the rest of my life and finished high school with some correspondence course. And say, Judge, don't you think that since the father of this child is off somewhere making a name for himself with his hot-pie high school diploma, that probably you ought to punish my boy here too while you're at it? I mean, don't you want to blame *him* a little too, Judge? I mean, maybe you think the school he'll go to ought to keep him out too, 'cause his mama's a fourteen-year-old girl? 'Course, Judge, I know I ain't got any rights, but it seems to me when that school I used to go to fixed it so I couldn't go there anymore, they punished me and my little boy too. Made it even tougher for him than it already is. So maybe that will make it easier for you, and you won't have to punish us any more. We already got it bad enough. Why don't you just go give another award to that beautiful school so they can hang it up on their wall.

"All right, Judge, I'm ready for you to sentence me. Only just remember, I never finished school like you did."

No simple theories explain the day-by-day, hour-by-hour experience of school. Something happens, and a teacher suddenly emerges as the most valuable human being in a child's life. Something else happens and there's not a teacher, guidance counselor or principal anywhere, it seems, who could reach that student exactly as the student must be reached. I sit in a homeroom of a school and watch the children go in and out. There's not a class in session; they merely wander in, speak a moment with a teacher who happens to be there and leave. Yet in these minutes I witness every human emotion, every human gesture. This one is seducing someone, this one's selling something, this one's angry, this one's adventurous, this one's ambitious, this one giggles, this one would cry given the chance, this one's so lonely looking he appears to be wrapped in cellophane, while that other one never walks more than six inches away from his friends. The teachers are the same. They're involved, bored, enthusiastic, cheered, duped, tired, disconsolate, hopeful, in love with some of the kids, turned away by some of the kids, outright hating some of the kids. I think sometimes as I watch them all moving about, flirting, hitting, talking, mumbling to themselves, that the miracle of the age is that order is achieved long enough to teach anybody a multiplication table. So much is going on in this one homeroom, it makes my head spin. I am exhausted by the sight of it, and I haven't spoken or even nodded to a single child.

One thing I can see in this homeroom is that many children are quite serious about school. They want to learn, they want to put in the effort. Another thing anyone can see is that many children cannot stand the hours they are forced to be here. They are racehorses in the starting gate, football players uniformed and ready to hit, waiting to be called onto the field.

Still another thing I see is mystery, uncertainty. I hold a strange belief when milling in train stations that every single person is caught in the midst of some marvelous dramatic adventure. Follow any of them, I tell an invisible journalist, and you'll uncover a great story. I feel this same way in a classroom or in the corridors of a school. Everyone has a delicious, poignant story to tell. They're holding it in, waiting for the right time to reveal it. Follow anyone of them, I tell myself, there must be something. Not merely a biography or a history, but some ongoing mystery, a caper being planned or even executed. The only reason that boy over there is quiet is because he's a genius or because he's plotting some incredible act. And that one there has secrets that, if they ever came to light, would shake this building and set back the school committee fifty years!

Dale McCutheon is the sixth of nine children. He is thirteen and in the eighth grade of his neighborhood public school. Dale is an extremely polite and obedient child who, it has always seemed to me, is especially frightened by displays of anger, even when the anger is not directed at him. He is not a particularly shy boy, but there are many sides to him that he keeps hidden; not just from me, but from his family as well. If, as I imagine, all the children in the halls of every school have their secrets, Dale's is that he is an eneuretic, a bed-wetter. It is for him and his family, and for his school too, a difficult and embarrassing problem. His brothers and sisters try to be serious about it, at least they have been cautioned to be serious and respectful by their parents, but it is sometimes hard for them to comply. Often Mr. and Mrs. McCutheon will be awakened by the giggling and yelling of children. "Dale did it again! Pee-yew. It *smells* in here. Mother, you have to change the sheets!" There will be more laughing and someone will try to hush the laughter and console Dale. Then one of the children will get angry at him, and before Mrs. McCutheon stumbles sleepily into the bedroom, one of the other children will spank the deeply ashamed and guilt-ridden boy.

For many years Dale's bed-wetting problem remained inside the family. While the McCutheons barely have enough money to live on, a special summer YMCA program made summer camp a possibility. Dale became terrified that his parents might send him and that he would be discovered. He has lived his entire life with the fear that one of his brothers or sisters might tell on him at school, and he would be ridiculed by the children in his class. In fact, the family secret was revealed to no one, except for several doctors, a priest, and a woman whose sister was a social worker. Everyone had ideas for the McCutheons, techniques that had always proved to stop bed-wetting, but nothing helped. But as long as their secret was kept and the boy continued on in school, perhaps, as everyone said, the problem would go away. One morning, Mrs. McCutheon would wake up and ask Dale, "Did you have a dry night?" And Dale would answer, "Yes, mother. I don't wet my bed anymore. Only babies do that." Then, instead of giving her the blank stare he gives everybody in the family when they wonder whether he has grown up, he would smile proudly and tell them he has become a man. At last the giggling and complaining at night would stop.

From the beginning, my friendship with Dale McCutheon was one of hunting for safe topics to speak about. He knew perfectly well that one of my intentions was to open up this precious secret, this package of shame. He sensed too how complicated the issue was for me. If I did not directly approach the subject, it might have meant that I was trying to be cautious and gentle. It also might have meant that I felt a bit queasy about it. My early caution only made matters worse. Still, on the few occasions when I tried to broach the subject directly—I had his parents' permission to do this—I received a blank stare. I don't ask you anything, and I don't hear anything until you find a safe topic, is what his face and body were telling me. So I would pull away from the bed-wetting, and Dale would relax as though nothing at all had been said.

Just how perplexing the matter of the bed-wetting was to me was made clear in a dream that I had some time after I met Dale:

I am in the school I have visited that day. In the midst of a crowd of students I select for no particular reason one boy. I tell myself he is the one I will ask to reveal the mysteries and adventures I am sure he harbors.

"You got secrets, kid?" I start, surprised by my rather abrupt manner. "Secrets you don't tell anybody in the whole world?"

"You better believe I do!" he answers.

"Yeah, like what kind of secrets you got on you today?" I ask.

"Today I got secrets about when everybody in the world's going to die."

"You mean you can tell me when I'm going to die?"

"The day, date, and minute, friend."

"You know when I'm going to die, and you're just walking here in the halls so quietly between. . ."

". . .between French class and social studies."

"Between French class and social studies?"

"Like I say, the day, date, and minute."

"Well, that surely is an impressive secret to be keeping in that head of yours, isn't it?"

"It is, indeed."

"Well, my friend, since you have this rather important bit of information about me, would you like to divulge it?"

"No, sir."

"You wouldn't eh? And why not, may I ask?"

"Because I would rather tell you the exact date of my own departure from this school."

"You're leaving? Why is that?" I ask.

"For me to know and for you to find out."

"Well, tell me this, when are you departing?"

"Next Monday at precisely 7:30 in the morning."

"You mean instead of coming to school, you're leaving?"

"Better believe it," he responds.

"Well, isn't this a bit sudden?"

"You wouldn't think so if you knew me."

"You mean I would have been able to see it coming?"

"Absolutely," he says.

"Well, will you come back?"

"I would presume not."

"You would presume not," I repeat.

"You heard me right."

"You're a bit pushy, aren't you," I say. "I mean, leaving school isn't something one is supposed to get so excited about, is it?"

"I'm not excited," he answers, totally unperturbed by my remark. "I'm taking the only course of action left. I'm departing."

"For good?"

"Quite possibly."

"And for good reason?" I am dying to learn the reason.

"Perhaps the finest reason in the world." Clearly, he has begun to enjoy baiting me.

"The finest reason in the world," I muse, "for leaving school. I've got it! You've graduated!"

"Nay sir. A long way from that. I'm only thirteen and when one is thirteen there is, unfortunately, not a single place in the world from which anyone can graduate."

"True enough. Well then you've flunked."

"You're a rude old man," he says, staring straight at me. "Perhaps the rudest I have ever known. My grades, sir, are of the top quality, perhaps the toppest quality."

"Your grades are good," I continue to calculate, "and you've not finished, so what can it be?"

"That's for me to know and for you to find out." He never moves away from me, a fact I construe as his wanting me to discover his secret.

"Would I be able to guess it merely by looking at you?" I ask.

"If you're truly insightful, sensitive, and compassionate."

"Oh," I smile, "the old I-S-O routine, eh?"

"*Pre*-cisely." He nods his head smartly exactly once.

"Well, given my I-S-O rating, I believe I have it."

"Say on," he goes.

"You, my dear young friend, are leaving school, possibly for good, though possibly not as well, next Monday morning at precisely 7:30 because everyone in this building, indeed everyone on these entire school grounds, the oldest teachers down to the youngest preschool toddlers, have learned that you wet your bed at night. You actually pee-pee in your sleep. Am I right?"

The young man again gives me his one smart nod of the head. "You bet your sweet ass big boy!"

It was a strange dream. There was no boy in the school I had visited who in any way resembled the boy in the dream. In fact, I knew no one resembling the dream boy. Eventually, I realized that it was Dale who had prompted the dream.

My dream was a source of personal enlightenment. The transformations of fact made it clear how perplexing the matter of the bedwetting was to me. The boy in the dream is articulate, eloquent even, a character from a nineteenth-century British novel about elite preparatory schools. That is, up until the end when, with his secret exposed, he becomes twentieth-century urban American. He has something on me, moreover, something of the most severe consequences: the date of my death. I treat him partly with respect, partly with condescension. I want him in school and dislike his snottiness, a quality, incidentally, that could not possibly be attributed to Dale McCutheon. The dream boy's plan to run away is what I always imagined Dale would do if he could; run away to a place and school, brothers and sisters who would never find out what he was and what he did, particularly at night.

Leaving at the precise hour of seven-thirty on Monday morning was reminiscent of two things in my own life. First is the railroad passenger image of escaping, going away for good, and the intense fear of people separating. Second, seven-thirty was the time my own father took my sister and me to school. I never left for school without a feeling of anxiety. It was the secret I had to keep from people, even my parents and sister who of course knew full well how frightened I was. As a boy Dale's age, my fright was enough to make me have to urinate. Had I been Dale McCutheon, and had someone come along inquiring about this fright, I no doubt would have stared at him blankly, as though I didn't know what in God's name he could be talking about.

Another thing about the dream: The dialogue is utterly false, an obvious caricature of real speech, and particularly of the sort of conversations Dale and I actually have. It reveals a peculiar stilted quality, but always, and this is the point, it remains perfectly controlled. Surprises surely are contained in the revelations, but one has the sense that neither of the participants will stray from their formal, polite, and controlled mannerisms. This was, for me, an essential ingredient of the dream. For in real life Dale and I, as any observer could discern, work to control our feelings, probably in the same way his brothers and sisters try to keep from laughing when they discover he has wet his bed. Dale cannot yet face the situation head on—one can easily understand this—and I cannot either. It is a delicate issue for a friend who is not his psychotherapist but rather someone who has intervened because of a recent development involving his school.

Early in his eighth grade year, the boys in Dale's class spent a long weekend on a country estate. It is the school's policy that every boy must go on this trip. No exceptions are made. The boys travel seven hours by bus, arriving at this forest area late in the afternoon. They pitch tents, arrange their supplies, and for three and a half days learn from their teachers how to live in such an environment. The program is not meant as a test of physical courage or stamina. Mountains may be climbed under the close watch of experienced men, but only if the boys elect to do so. Sports are permitted only in the evenings after dinner. The days are spent foraging for food and learning how to live off the land.

Most of the boys adore the experience. It far exceeds anything they do inside the old school building back in the city. Some apply for junior counselor positions for future trips. Many boys, naturally, dislike the excursion. They treat it as an interminable ordeal. Dale McCutheon dreaded the trip as early as fifth grade. The moment he heard that it was compulsory, he became panic-stricken. For two and a half years he held in the back of his mind the possibility that he would be unable to control himself for the three nights he would be away. Perhaps the problem would vanish by then, he thought. Or maybe by the time he reached the eighth grade the trip would no longer be compulsory.

The two and a half years finally passed with no changes in the school's policy. Several times Mrs. McCutheon asked the school administration whether her son had to go. She was advised that *all* boys make the trip. Mr. McCutheon believed in the idea of such an excursion. Perhaps several days with men only would change his son, he argued. The family by this time was more than a trifle angry with Dale. It seemed to them the problem should have gone away by now. He was thirteen, and surely no one his age wet his bed at night. Dale begged his mother to keep him home, but eventually he boarded the bus with the other boys. Some of them noticed his fright and kidded him for being a baby afraid to leave his mommy. Dale did his best to conceal his terror.

Miraculously, to Dale, there was no problem the first night of the excursion. He woke several times and cautiously felt around his waist, but everything was dry. The next day his spirits were high. He enjoyed learning how to make food from wild plants and classify mushrooms. The secret he had carried for so long seemingly had vanished.

It was different the second night. He did not awake until morning when the sounds of boys talking and laughing startled him. The two boys sharing his tent had discovered the wetness. They hounded Dale mercilessly, and he wept. Only then did they leave him alone, but not until they agreed that one of the senior people had to be told. Dale begged his friends not to say anything, but the boys insisted. The counselors, who were teachers and coaches in the school, were advised of the problem. Two of them lectured Dale on the seriousness of his condition. They could barely hide their incredulity. They didn't know whether to take him home or let him stay the weekend. On his urging they agreed to let him remain. He promised he would stay awake all the next night to prevent a recurrence. "Aren't you old for this?" they asked him again and again. When he stared at them they shook him by the shoulders and told him he was a very sick young man. He pretended not to hear them and they were confused by his begging them one moment and total silence the next.

After his session with the counselors Dale heard them talking about him. He heard them laughing too, and calling him "the pisser." He listened to them make jokes about his urinating on the other boys, who now demanded that they be moved out of Dale's tent. It wasn't fair, they joked and pleaded. You never know who might get hit by it. The senior counselor insisted that they remain with Dale. It will give him confidence, he told them. He also scolded them for laughing, but the boys detected that like them, the older men found the situation amusing.

It was hours before Dale could show his face. When finally he saw the others at lunch he sensed that the whole group would laugh at him. But nobody said a word. Many of the boys looked at him peculiarly, but nothing was said. The first break in their silence came that night when they were preparing for bed and someone muttered that "McCutheon wouldn't have to go piss behind a tree. He'll probably just save it up for Grummond and Toomey," the boys who slept near him. Those hearing the remark exploded with laughter as though they had kept in their feelings as long as they could. The joking would have continued had not a counselor chastised the boys.

Dale was humiliated. His face felt hot, and his entire body began to perspire. He wanted to run away. What would he do on returning to school? It was all over now. There would be no more getting along with the boys even though there was no possibility of an accident occurring during the day. There never had been one before. It was only at night that things happened. The girls in his class would be told too. They would probably know the minute the bus returned. And everybody would tell their parents, which meant that his own parents would hear of the accident on the outing. He crawled into his sleeping bag, which smelled from urine, and began his all-night vigil. The other boys in the tent kept silent. He could feel them looking at him. Suddenly they began to cough and wheeze as though they were being choked by an odor. When the boys in other tents heard the coughing they too began to cough and laugh. Soon the entire camp was laughing and wheezing. It took several minutes for the counselors to shout down the boys. One of the older men entered Dale's tent and told Peter Grummond and Johnny Toomey that their behavior was childish and that they had better put an end to it immediately or he'd make them stay up all night and freeze. The boys said nothing. The counselor asked Dale if he was all right. Dale didn't answer. The man made sure he was covered. By then the boy's pillow was wet with tears.

Despite his efforts to stay awake, Dale fell asleep for short stretches. Each time he awoke suddenly and prayed that his sleeping bag was dry. The night passed without an accident. He felt relieved when morning came, but he knew it was too late to undo the situation. Everyone was talking about him now. They asked each other whether McCutheon had drowned anyone last night and made deals so they wouldn't have to sit near him on the bus going home. When someone suggested the boys go swimming, it opened the door for still more razzing and joking. "Can you wash off the yellow?" they laughed. "Ring around the collar. Ring around the collar." "The pisser strikes again." "Keep McCutheon out of the water and fight pollution." This line even broke up some of the counselors.

Dale took a walk in the woods across from the lake. No one joined him. The plan he had schemed the night before would have to go into effect. He would make his parents transfer him to another school, or he would quit. He could not face the boys again. Even if the problem went away for good, he would not return to the same school. He would go to jail first.

In the woods Dale heard the boys playing along the lake's shore trying to stoke up their courage to jump into the icy water. He could not see them, but their voices carried through the trees. Walking alone, a fantasy ran through his head, one that he later recounted to me.

He is in a courtroom standing before a judge. His crime is being a bed-wetter. The judge wears a white wig, just as Dale had seen English judges wear in movies. He sits on a chair high above the courtroom and peers down at Dale. The boy's neck aches from having to keep looking up at him.

"We have decided to sentence you," the judge begins, "because as you know, you have committed a serious crime. And do you know what the crime is?"

"I urinated in my sleeping bag when I wasn't supposed to, your honor." Everyone in the gallery begins to laugh. The audience is composed entirely of adults. None of Dale's schoolmates are present. He sees his parents, but his brothers and sisters are not in the courtroom. His mother is crying. She keeps wiping her eyes with the light blue handkerchief Dale had once given her as a Christmas present. His father is half comforting his wife, half rooting for the judge to hand down a stiff penalty to his son. "It's gone on too long," Dale hears his father grumbling. "It's gone on too long."

"Well, son," the judge resumes, "I'm afraid I must pass down a very harsh penalty. Either you cannot ever go to school again or you must go to prison for ten years and then you must go back to school." The audience groans. Dale's father seems pleased. Apparently, this is what he wanted. But Dale is delighted.

"Do I tell you now?" he asks the judge, peering up at him.

"Yes, you must."

"Okay. I'll never go to school again!" Dale smiles; the audience is shocked.

The trip home in the bus was an excruciating experience. Despite warnings from the counselors, the boys continued to call Dale "the Pisser" and jeered at him. Those obliged to sit near him pretended he carried a contagious disease. They glanced down at his groin as though waiting for him to have an accident. People kept shouting that everyone should put on a raincoat just in case. When someone tried to be helpful, the other boys only pushed him away and accused him of having the same problem. "Hey, if we let the pissers get together they'll flood us out of here," the tougher boys roared. No amount of remonstrating by the counselors could quiet them.

Dale never told his parents about the weekend's problems. When they asked whether everything had gone all right, he answered yes. When he saw their relief, any thought he had of revealing the incident vanished. But he refused to go to school for two days on the excuse that he was sick. His mother kept him home. When he protested on the third day, she insisted there was nothing wrong with him and that he had to go. A younger sister, Abby, accompanied him. By this point Mrs. McCutheon suspected that something had gone wrong on the excursion. Amazingly, with so many children at school talking about the bed-wetting incident, not one of the McCutheon children heard the news. But by the end of the week Abby had learned of Dale's accident.

The McCutheons were furious with Dale but surprised that the school had said nothing to them. They did not know whether to be thankful that nothing had come of it or wish that perhaps the school could intervene and end their problem, once and for all. When they approached Dale with the story Abby had reported, he met them with his blank stare. Not even a whipping by his father could get him to admit what had happened. His mother now understood his reason for staying home from school. "I should have known," she told her son repeatedly, and now with a tone that made him believe she had at last quit on him. There was nothing to do, however, but keep Dale in school and hope that in a short time the students would find something else to talk about. Abby demanded that Dale stop going to the school. She was getting razzed, she sobbed. It wasn't fair that Dale was ruining everything for her too.

Mrs. McCutheon didn't know how to respond. Mr. McCutheon felt his daughter's request was just. Dale, he shouted, was ruining the whole family. The only solution was to put him in some kind of an institution. Mrs. McCutheon seemed willing to listen to the proposition. Abby, however, got scared by this idea and suggested that they talk about it in front of Dale. The boy, in the meanwhile, just stared into space.

There were long discussions that weekend. Included in some of them, I offered to arrange for psychiatric treatment for Dale as a way of making certain he would remain in school. More importantly, I argued, it was essential that Dale not be sent to any mental hospital or special institution. Mr. and Mrs. McCutheon listened to me, but they remained unconvinced. Abby felt guilty about what she had said. None of the McCutheon children wanted Dale to leave home. "It's just not going to go on," Mr. McCutheon promised bitterly. "I'll guarantee you that. Up to here. I'm up to here with that kid," he poked at his neck, "and that baby thing he's got going there. I'm waiting for the school to throw him out. That'll come, you know. They'll throw him out. Then we'll see what he'll do. Thirteen years old. My God!"

I saw Mrs. McCutheon, looking troubled, standing behind her husband. She wore that expression that said she couldn't go on. I had seen it a million times. "It's going to be all right," I said. "I don't know why, but I've got a good feeling about it." All of the McCutheons heard my wishful thoughts. They knew there was nothing I could do to make "the problem" disappear. Abby, though, was counting on me. She sent me notes during the next week and telephoned once to learn whether I had come up with a plan. I told her I had selected a doctor for Dale if he wanted to talk to someone. She was disappointed. The matter for her had to be resolved at that instant. Nothing less would satisfy her. Part of me felt the same way.

Two weeks after the weekend excursion, the principal of Dale's school, Samuel T. Clarendon, telephoned the McCutheons. He asked to meet with them at once. Mr. McCutheon refused to go to the school. As a grown man, he said, he could not stomach the idea of talking with another grown man about a thirteen-year-old boy who wet his bed. Mrs. McCutheon was irritated by her husband's refusal, but she understood it. It was a situation she had faced over and over again. There was always someone reacting violently to Dale's condition and walking away from it. She was the sole person who remained constant. I could hardly refuse when she requested that I accompany her to Mr. Clarendon's office, where she introduced me as "a close friend of the family, almost a relative." I was touched by her words, but, admittedly, there was something in me that resonated with Mr. McCutheon's sentiments as well. Men, I thought, listening to the principal, hold special attitudes about incontinence, and the lack of control generally. Even the most mature men may smirk when hearing about a bed-wetter. It is not like a language deficiency or physical violence in the classroom. Bed-wetting is too close to home. Any man can put himself in Dale McCutheon's shoes as easily as he can put himself in the shoes of any of Dale's friends, or former friends. It may be hard to admit these feelings, but they are there.

Samuel Clarendon was not smirking. He wasted no time outlining the seriousness of Dale's troubles, for the boy as well as for the school.

Throughout his remarks Mrs. McCutheon just nodded. It looked to me as if she would have nodded yes to anything he said. We have decided that you should wait three nights, Mrs. McCutheon. If the boy hasn't stopped wetting his bed by then, drag him into the attic and shoot him! And she probably would have nodded yes to this. I couldn't believe her abiding by his every word.

"Here it is in a nutshell," Mr. Clarendon was saying. "We had this thing, this episode on the excursion, and there's nothing anybody can do to set all that straight again. I wish to God we could but we can't. You should have spelled out the situation for us, Mrs. McCutheon, and we could have taken his name off the list. Anyway, what's done is done. But now we still have the problem of . . ."

"The other kids . . ." Mrs. McCutheon interrupted him, nodding all the time.

"No, no, no," the principal corrected her. "Not the other kids at all. They'll probably forget the whole thing in another week or so." He leaned back in his chair. "No, it's not the kids. It's Dale's teachers." Both of us must have looked confused. "The teachers, sure," he repeated. "We can't let this kind of thing happen. You know . . ."

"What kind of thing?" I broke in.

"His nighttime affair."

"His bed-wetting," I said bluntly. Mrs. McCutheon was watching us, wanting me, I assumed, to bring the issue out in the open and call it by its real name. But she continued nodding in response to everyone of the principal's utterances.

"His bed-wetting," Mr. Clarendon said. "How do we know he won't just, you know, pop off at any time in one of his classes?"

"Pop off in one of his . . . Mr. Clarendon," I began angrily, "do you know what you just said?"

"I most certainly do," he anwered gruffly.

"You said he may wet his pants during the day, in one of his classes." I could see what lay ahead. Dale obviously had been suspended. Mrs. McCutheon did not understand this yet, and I was trying to break into the ridiculous premise of the suspension before the principal pronounced the words, he can't return to this school.

"That's what I said," Mr. Clarendon responded in a take it or leave it manner.

"You can't be serious."

"Are you a lawyer, Mr. Cottle?"

"No, but I'm afraid that what you're leading up to is going to make us get one. I don't believe . . . you actually think this boy is going to do something during the *day*? First of all, his problem's almost over now, and it doesn't ever happen during the day. It happens at *night*. Not in the *day*. Right, Mrs. McCutheon?" For the first time she nodded strenuously for *our* side. "It's not a day problem. There aren't any more excursions anyway, so what's the risk? Why can't you keep him in?"

"We can't take chances."

"What kind of chances are you taking? Has he ever wet his pants once in school?"

"We just can't take chances. That's all." By now Mr. Clarendon was more than merely impatient with me. He looked at the clock and made other gestures to signify his desire to be done with both of us.

"Listen, don't rush this," I challenged him. "You can't stop him from going to school."

"You're absolutely right," he said to me sternly. "I can't stop him from going to school. But I *can* stop him from going to *this* school, and that's exactly what I'm doing. The boy's out for one month," he announced to Mrs. McCutheon, "or until a time that you can prove to us that he is able to control himself, night *and* day!" This last was meant for me. It came with a long hard stare.

"Is seeing a psychiatrist enough for you?" I asked, my anger not receding an inch.

"It is if the psychiatrist sends me an official letter guaranteeing that the boy . . ."

"I know," I muttered, "won't *pop* off in the middle of English class."

"You know, Mrs. McCutheon," the principal said with sudden quietness, "you and I might have been able to settle this matter more easily without your friend being here."

Mrs. McCutheon nodded. I whispered an apology to both of them. "Well, that's that" were the last words I remember the principal saying. I don't recall Mrs. McCutheon speaking again, although she did say thank you when she left his office.

Outside in the main hall with the students making as much noise as they could until a man rushed out of an office and threatened them with something called a work-study if they didn't quiet down, I saw Mrs. McCutheon start to cry.

"We'll fix it," I tried to comfort her. She shook her head. I felt horrible about the way I had acted in the principal's office. Selfishly I wondered whether Mrs. McCutheon could have believed I was responsible for the suspension. "I saw that damn decision coming a mile away," I said, hoping to justify my behavior.

"I saw that suspension," she replied, "the moment we entered that office. That man suspends children. I saw it in his face. I saw it in the way he keeps that desk of his. Everything so neat. Nothing out of line, you know what I mean? That's a man who never once got up in the middle of the night with a crying child. He never once cleaned the rear end *or* front end of a soiled baby. He'd beat a child before he'd clean him. Believe me, I know. All I had to do was see his desk and the way he had his whole office looking so neat."

We had reached the front door of the school. Mrs. McCutheon looked to be perfectly composed, but once outside she broke down again and cried. We walked around the block before going home.

"What do we do?" she asked over and over again. "They don't want him and there's no way of knowing how long he'll be like this. I've read books on it. Everybody says it disappears. But when's that going to be? How do we know he might not be too old for school by the time he's cured? What's going to be worse for him, being a bed-wetter or a boy without a proper education? You think people like Clarendon ever think of that?"

"You agree, though, with their position, don't you Mrs. McCutheon? You think it's all right for them to throw Dale out for this?" I wanted to build up some fighting strength in her, as if she needed my prodding.

"I think it's dreadful what they're doing. You know exactly how I feel. But they got their rights too. They can't be wiping up children old enough to be caring for themselves and trying to teach all at the same time. You know that. They're not supposed to be mothers or maids in that school. That's not what they're trained for. They're supposed to be helping these children with their minds, not washing out their underwear for them."

"You sound like you're giving up," I said with childlike disappointment in my voice.

"And suppose you tell me just what I'm supposed to do. Send him to a private school? With what? Take him to see some fancy psychiatrist like you were saying in there? With what? His father says put him in a hospital. Even if I wanted to we couldn't do that either with the little bit of money we have. He's *not* the only child I've got, you know. He's not the only mouth sitting there at my table each night to feed. He may be the biggest problem we've got at this moment, but he's not the only one. You know, you can go in there and shout it out with that clean desk man, that Mr. Clean there, so orderly and all. But I know what he's facing a whole lot better than you do. He's got a bunch of kids running around in that school the same as I got running around in my house. You can't afford the time or the effort or the money to all of a sudden stop with everything you're doing and pay attention to just one of them. The world doesn't work that way. You might like it to, but it doesn't. I don't like getting up at night, twice some nights for your information, and going in to clean up that smelly mess he makes. I don't like it, but I do it. Clarendon doesn't like doing it to any child for any reason. But he's got no choice. Someone cleans up for the bed-wetter, everybody else screams and cries and bellyaches all over the place, and somebody has to suspend children who don't fit the bill. That's his job. Your job is to argue, his job is to throw out the bad apples. My job's like every other mother's job. We clean up the mess and make sure nobody's upset by the smell and see if we can't patch up little children's hearts and put tym back in bed and help them to go to sleep.

"You want to tell me that man has no right to keep Dale out of school? Of course he has no right. By law, Dale *has* to stay in school. But what's the law? A piece of paper? Some words somebody in the legislature wrote down? A boy who wets his bed," she recited in a caricatured tone, "has the same right to go to school as a boy who doesn't wet his bed. That's what the law says. What the school says is that this boy is a damn nuisance. Let his parents handle him. Let his mother clean him up. We're not going to do it!

"You know what that Clarendon man is really saying? He's saying start all over again, Mrs. McCutheon. That's what he's saying. Start all over again. You did lousy with that boy of yours. Thirteen years old, and he wets his bed three and four times a week. You did plenty lousy. Don't go asking us to mend all the mistakes you made. Don't go thinking we're getting paid to do the job you never could do. *That's* what Mr. Neat Desk Clarendon in there is saying."

"And you agree with that?"

"I don't have a choice." Mrs. McCutheon looked at me as we walked in the direction of her home. "I don't have any choice in this one at all. He's not going to pick up where I failed. No one is. Not even you. I'm the one who picks up where I failed."

"Dale's problem isn't your failure," I said as gently as possible.

"What the hell's the difference whose failure it is?" she said impatiently. "So it's not my failure. So it's somebody else's failure. You want to know something? It's Clarendon's failure too. What do you think of that? An hour ago it wasn't but now he's in it just as much as we are. We're stuck with the daytime and nighttime routines. But now he's in it because he wants to ignore it, get rid of it. I tell you, he's Mr.

Clean. He doesn't want to touch the dirty linens or smell them any more than anyone else does. He throws the boy out of school. My husband says put him away, hide him somewhere in the basement of a mental hospital in Waltham. You say get him a psychiatrist. A lawyer says pass a law. Even my daughter—you remember last week—big deal that she is, now she's sounding like maybe we should kill the boy because it's starting to damage *her* reputation. Miss America. Her big-shot seventh-grade reputation.

"See what I mean? Everybody's pushing and shoving Dale, here, there, in school, out of school, but who's got the advice for me? What do I do with him? What do I do with myself? I've got some feelings too, you know. Not many after all these years, but I've got a little pride left. It's no picnic, you know, being the mother of a bed-wetting thirteen-year-old boy who they just threw out of school. My husband will be delighted to hear that. And don't think for a minute he isn't hurt by all this too. Fifty years old, and he's got this to contend with on top of everything else. He hasn't had it so easy either, you know. All *you* see is his anger but he's plenty hurt. Plenty. What do you think a man feels when his son wets his bed every night? You think he feels good about it? He doesn't know whether to laugh or cry, kill the boy or himself."

"Mrs. McCutheon," I asked when I saw she had stopped, "would you like us to get you a lawyer for this school thing?"

Mrs. McCutheon's eyes were perfectly clear, and something about her walk made me think that she had recovered her second wind, or some hidden strength. She looked straight ahead. "Who'll pay for this lawyer?" she asked smartly.

"We will," I answered.

"Then get one!"

"And someone for Dale? You know, to talk to maybe?"

"Who'll pay for that?"

"We will."

"Then I'll take one of those too," she grinned.

"And I'll buy you a cup of coffee."

"And I think you will too," she nodded, still looking straight ahead.

3.

The Evils of Testing and Tracking

This morning, I walked down the halls of a Boston area public school. The atmosphere in the school, that intangible quality that observers of education always mention, was difficult to describe. The children were in their classrooms running around or sitting at their desks. In one room there was utter chaos, in another room there was an uncanny sense of order and obedience. In still another room, a group of about ten children, perhaps eight or nine years old, huddled together on a green rug. They sat at the foot of a young man and looked up at him as though he were imparting the world's secrets. How the children seemed to love that teacher. Outside their classroom a small sign was taped to the blond oak door. It read: "Shh—we're testing in here."

It seemed pleasant enough in that room, not at all the scene I usually find in the schoolrooms I visit. Indeed, in one of Boston's inner-city schools I witnessed a very different scene in a room where another sign indicated that testing was going on. In that school I watched a child sit for more than fifteen minutes—it seemed like a century—refusing to answer even one question her tester was putting to her. The tester, an older woman, seemed patient enough, but it was evident that this child wasn't about to speak. It was also clear that the child was so terrified she might not have been able to speak if she had wanted to. She stared at the tester, her eyes rarely blinking, and with each new question or request she swallowed, opened her eyes as wide as she could, and smiled just slightly.

After fifteen minutes of this tortured routine, the tester gave in and excused the child. The girl stood up, opened her eyes wide, and walked slowly from the room. Outside in the hall she began to run, and disobeying the signs to walk at all times, she practically flew up the stairs at the end of the corridor, smack into a friend. At once she was explaining her testing session with the friend, and in an instant the two of them were laughing hysterically and darting up the stairs together. That same day that little ten-year-old girl had the following statement entered in her official school record: "The child's IQ is so low she is untestable. Recommendation: Special class work is required, probably not in this school."

Several months later the girl was out of school. Unable to find her a special class or special school, her mother and father let her "drop out" for a while. A few people, however, felt the girl to be testable, even bright, even special, and this time a young psychologist was brought in to test the girl. As it was late spring the psychologist took the girl and the testing equipment outdoors. They talked together for almost an hour about all sorts of things and then, after explaining the testing procedures, the psychologist began to test. The final accounting showed an I.Q. of 115: The child's verbal ability was outstanding; her weaknesses were reading comprehension and arithmetic. So a tutor was provided for the girl in arithmetic and reading comprehension. One year later she was tested again, this time by one of the school's guidance counselors. Her IQ was now 124. In the fall of that year the little girl was admitted to a voluntary busing program, and now she attends the rather nice suburban school I visited this morning where the other children say, "She's neat, except when she talks too much!"

A few years ago a major topic of debate in America's schools was the issue of tests and testing. A variety of tests came under examination, not merely ones measuring intelligence. The so-called progressive movement in education argued that the act of testing was itself inhuman, unnecessary, and often a substitute for genuine learning. It claimed that when teachers had little to say they tested their students. There were also those persons, who, while sympathetic to the need for educational reform, nonetheless wondered how children could be fairly placed in the best type of classroom groupings without the use of tests. The psychological reformers implicitly agreed. If one wants to honor psychic problems, understand children, and diagnose their conditions, one had better test, gently of course, but still test.

Then came the debates on intelligence and the startling question of whether or not existing intelligence tests even measured intelligence. In 1969 David Wechsler, the creator of perhaps the most well-known intelligence measure, told an audience at the University of Illinois that he did not know what intelligence was. Nor was he certain what his test actually measured.

At the time of Wechsler's presentation, debates on testing were focused on the issue of whether the intelligence tests used in most schools were culture free. The likelihood that they were, in fact, biased in favor of white, middle- and upper-class people was reinforced by the experimenter expectancy phenomenon demonstrated by Professor Robert Rosenthal and his associates at Harvard. The bias of a test, therefore, coupled with the expectations of white examiners, hardly afforded black children or poor children much of a chance to fare too well. There was of course the "exceptional" black child, the one in four or eight or ten who scored high on some test and jumped into all sorts of advantageous positions in his or her school. But the advancement of this one child merely replicated the form of advancement America always allowed its minorities. One in six or eight is typically permitted to make it through, especially if they can score well on established tests.

Eventually the testing debate carried into another sacred realm of human potential, namely, the inheritability of intelligence. This new debate carried with it an assumption that intelligence tests are valid and offer appropriate information for exploring the question of why some of us are "born smart" and others of us are not. The debate also caused many educators to reexamine the data on intelligence testing, particularly studies on twins, since the inheritability factor is best observed in this way.

Throughout the changing controversy and irrespective of how particular studies turned out, testing in America's public schools has gone on and on. Every child is tested, and parents, teachers, and administrators accept the results of these cognitive and psychological measures as the ultimate truth. While we all seem to recognize the import of whatever debate is raging, we nonetheless reify test results, even when experts like Wechsler publicly state that no one yet knows what intelligence truly is. So, for a society that doesn't know what "it" is, we have never stopped categorizing, grouping, liking, loving, and generally treating people because of their measured amount of "it." Even after debunking some test or waging war against the idea of testing, I will still say, "Well, here's a kid flunking English, and he's got an IQ of 125 at least." The person *has* to be "smart," because the very test I oppose has proven it.

It goes without saying that the great advantage held by many of those who debate the values of IQ tests, all tests for that matter, is that they never have to know the children and young adults whose lives are affected by their tests and theories. Granted, much of our research work must be done under isolated, even sanitized conditions; personal feelings and human interactions "spoil" experimental results. But when people come along and make their bold pronouncements about what education should be or shouldn't be, and how tests do this or that, or even proclaim that school doesn't matter, I wonder whether these people ever talk with the children in America's schools or stay associated with schools long enough to follow the lives of any students. After ten years of observing schools, most of them in poor urban areas, and most of them run under the worst possible conditions, I have come to know a group of young people and their families, and have watched closely what tests and the whole testing procedure does to these children. I recall speaking with a group of four black boys in the fourth grade of a Philadelphia school some three or four years back. Here is something of that conversation.

"There ain't no fair test no black kid's ever going to get from no white man or white woman. They put grades on those tests. We behave good, they give us extra points. We bad mouth 'em, like if we did something to them once they didn't like, they take the points away from us.

"Only reason they give us those tests is so that they can make us look bad to one another. Law says they got to give the tests, so they give the tests. Man told my mother that I couldn't read. He said the test showed I couldn't read. Test didn't have nothing about reading in it, so how'd he know I couldn't read. So my mother says, Bernard says the test wasn't on reading. So the man says you want to see the test? So she says yes, and here's this big part on the test about reading, you know, and remembering what you're reading, but they never gave me that part 'cause I'd have remembered. I ain't saying I read fast, but I'd have remembered. Just 'cause your lips move when you read don't mean you don't remember.

"My older sister she took this test they gave her with this other girl. See what I mean? All of 'em were supposed to be getting this test, whatever it was for, individual, but they made her take it with this other girl. So while the test is going on, my sister's trying to answer the questions but the teacher ain't giving her the chance. She keeps telling my sister, you're next, you're next. So my sister waits for the other girl to be done, keeps her mouth shut, being polite, but when the other girl is done, the teacher don't come back to my sister. She says we're done. So my sister thinks they didn't have no time and that she'll have to be tested another day, which kind of makes her nervous all over again. But there ain't no other day, man. She's had it. That was it.

All they say is she's doing a whole lot better. That's what they told my parents. Told *her* too. But they never even tested her. But see, all they wanted to do was make everybody think she'd been tested. They weren't going to do nothing for her anyway. Hell, she'll be in the bottom track of this school 'til the day she dies."

"And you're going to be with her," his buddies teased him.

"That's what you think," he defended himself. "When they test me they're going to find out I'm a genius, and they're going to say, Man, you're a genius, you got points to give away. Give away all those IQ points, man. Somebody gave you way too many."

"Day you got too many points, man, is the day I'm going to be principal of this school."

We need not pause too long on the old issue that those children who live with hierarchical divisions in their lives—and certainly testing produces hierarchies—are the children tested the most. Conversely those children who by token of their social standing and lifelong chain of opportunities, those who suffer the least careerwise, though not necessarily emotionally, are those likely to attend schools where testing is relied on to a lesser degree. This is not, of course, always true. One of the dreadful realities of the progressive education movement, a movement that reached its peak long before debates over the biases of intelligence tests reached public consciousness, was that while progressive education deemphasized intelligence testing, it drowned students in psychological and aptitude tests. One found in the 1940s and 1950s a group of wealthy children in progressive schools, less concerned with their IQ's than with the results of the Rorschach, Thematic Apperception and Kuder Preference tests that had been administered to them.

Those of us who attended progressive schools at this time rarely thought much about IQ scores. We did, of course, rate one another (and from time to time, probably, hate one another) on the basis of revealed intelligence. These were the messages of the tests we received the instant we entered kindergarten. One cannot forget that no matter how much test results are derogated or ignored, their mere presence even in a locked file cabinet in a run-down warehouse in a quarantined part of a town bespeaks their importance to individuals and those who assess them and ultimately determine their next educational step. If intelligence and psychological tests weren't important, we used to argue, then why did we have to sit in those rooms and fill out those forms?

Something else troubled us. If someone were testing us for

something, were they not in effect suspicious of that something? If they studied our blood, surely, they were hunting for disease. If they administered us a psychological test or made us visit a guidance counselor, then somebody had noticed something that was not quite right. Did intelligence tests mean, therefore, that people were questioning our intelligence, disapproving of us, or merely wanting to clump us with those they thought we would get along with better? Or was it that they wanted to keep those they believed weren't so smart segregated from those they believed really were.

Any test has the power to affect one's self-image, for the good if one is lucky enough to be "scientifically" deemed brilliant, ingenious, intelligent. More importantly, test results underwrite and decide the educational fate of entire human groups. Like tattoos, test scores remain permanent marks of one's capacities and chances.

The students in a small industrial town in the western part of Massachusetts knew this. I met with several white middle-class juniors at the town's main public high school on several occasions. On one rainy afternoon in the front entrance of their school, a young woman told me the following story.

"Georgia Willows," she began, "was in my class ever since kindergarten. I never liked her too much, but I had to see her all the time 'cause our parents were friends. I remember she lived in this real large house. We used to play there. Georgia always thought she was the smartest girl in the world. God's gift, you know. By the time we were in grammar school everybody considered her the smartest girl in the school. She acted that way too. I didn't really think lots of people liked her. You know how kids always talk about who's the smartest in their class and stuff like that? We always talked about her as being the smartest—she and this boy whose family moved away. They were the smartest by far.

"Then last year this other girl visited the school on one of these exchange programs, you know, from Holland, and not only was she gorgeous, she was even smarter than Georgia. I mean she was incredible. I think she spoke about six languages. She'd never even been in America before, and she spoke better than I do. And she'd read all these books I hadn't even heard of, American books! So Georgia really had someone to compete with. When the boy left, she thought she was going to be the queen all by herself, but then this Stephanie comes and Georgia goes crazy. I mean she really got upset. There was this one time that she was over at our house when her parents were visiting and all of a sudden she starts to cry. We're up in my room, you know, and out of the clear blue she's crying. And she keeps saying, if I'm not the smartest person in our class I don't want to be alive. I told her she was crazy to take the whole thing so seriously. Besides, this other girl was going back to Holland at the end of the year. But she didn't care. She didn't even listen to me. She just said she wanted to know Stephanie's IQ and if it was higher than her's she'd have to die.

"I didn't think she was serious about it, but she was. Just before Easter she killed herself. Her mother told my mother that she never got over not being the smartest, no matter what anybody said to her. She killed herself. I never knew anybody before that had ever done that. I think if IQ means that much to someone there must be something wrong. But maybe there's something with testing people and making them think how smart they are is the most important thing in their lives. Either they shouldn't test us or they shouldn't tell us what we did on the tests. I suppose that's no good. They have to tell. So maybe they just shouldn't test. Maybe their problem is that all they want to do is test people without remembering to treat us like human beings instead of test scores!"

In that same school, the issue of testing was discussed by a young man, who, that very week, had learned of his own performance on a set of standardized achievement tests.

"I try not to compare myself with anybody," he began, "but kids talk. Everybody says they aren't going to tell anybody what they got, but like, in about five minutes everybody knows. Some mystery. I was thinking about tests and all that the other day, and I decided that there's only one way to get rid of them, which they should, 'cause they only make people anxious. If you eliminate money in our society, you could eliminate tests and all these test scores. See, to be American means that you have to have a lot of money. No matter what you earn, you aren't satisfied until you have more than the next guy. That's the same thing with tests. Giving us our score isn't enough. They have to give us the percentile reading as well. Nobody's supposed to get like a 690 and think they're really special. Guidance counselor tells them right away that 690 may sound good, but its only the eightieth percentile. You got to have money, and you got to have IQ points, and PSAT points and SAT points. Americans love numbers and quantities. Big's the name of the game. Produce and get bigger. Inches, pounds, dollars, points on tests, that's all anybody cares about, even the minority students in our school. Nobody asks them whether they're happy. All people want to know is whether their achievement scores have gone up or how many points they scored in a basketball game.

"Maybe what they ought to do is establish these IQ banks. If you got a low IQ you go to the bank and take out a loan. One guy wants fifteen points so you give it to him at 8½ percent. Sure would be easier than sitting in a counselor's office for an hour trying to explain why you did so poorly on some test or trying to convince him that while you're only in the eightieth percentile you're far and away the smartest eightieth percentile guy going. I figure I'll make a million either opening up IQ banks all over the country or making these little necklaces people could wear with their IQs carved in them. Instead of faking your modesty about your IQ or PSAT you could have it inscribed in your jewelry. Unless of course you're really a dummy, in which case we could just lie with the jewelry. That's another thing, we don't have any good way of defining someone as a dummy. And who really cares whether they care or not."

Let us be reminded that while some among us debate tests, their use and value as well as their political, psychological and educational implications, a far larger group continues to take these tests and be influenced by them, whether they believe in them or not. Test results may determine children's destinies; raw scores and standard deviations are translated into educational levels, psychological labels and diagnoses, and positions in academic tracks. As much as we might like to deny the fact, very few children will rise from the track in which they are placed when they are very young. Human interaction after all, and that includes our evaluations of one another, is based in great measure on the way we account for events and actions. A great hitter smashes a home run, and we say, what did you expect? A poor hitter does the same, and we say he got lucky. A poor black child scores high on an intelligence test, and we say he's a freak of nature. He does poorly, and we are relieved that he affirms our expectations. Through personal experience, and again through the investigations of Professor Rosenthal, we know how significant our expectations become for another person's self-concept and ultimately his or her performance.

American schools have always advertised that doing well and being smart can earn students heavenly opportunities at some point in their academic career. Years ago the term "late bloomer" alerted us to the many "last" chances certain students possess. It was a valuable term and significant for those who believed the course of life was arranged by the third, fourth, or fifth year. I remember being appalled to learn that a foreign country valuing education had resigned itself to sorting out its college-bound students from the rest of the pack as early as third grade. The experts and politicians lamented that the society could not afford to have all children attend college and professional schools. A cutoff had to be made. Relying on intelligence and aptitude testing, the published statements from the country's Ministry of Education assured any critic that the child's capacities could be measured at age seven, eight, nine, and ten. Why, then, bother to nurture low scorers when space was limited?

At least we didn't have *that* in our country, I remember thinking. Here, every person can graduate from high school, for whatever that means. True enough, but there have always been high school graduates and high school graduates. The poor, and especially poor black children, sustain the most hurtful and crippling blows from intelligence and psychological testing. We do, indeed, have children who, very early, are placed in custodial educational institutions where they are guarded until the law says we can legitimately quit on them, which, in fact, is what we have done from the beginning. No one is openly malevolent toward these children. We do the best we can with what we have. I have uttered this phrase a million times. Sometimes the words "with what we have" refers to our own capabilities, our patience, and sense of optimism. Sometimes it refers to the students in our classes, those put there by administrative action, fate, a computer. Yet underlying it all is that intelligence test score or psychological diagnostic.

We live in a moment when tests determine not merely in which class a child will learn mathematics, but how far and in what ways that child will move, in the world, in his or her mind. When in doubt, we test; when documentation of our preconceptions and prejudgments is required, we test. To demonstrate our successes or our policies gone awry, we test. It is an actuarial flow chart that the coaches and managers of education consult, the very chart that Professor Rosenthal recontextualized when he employed the same currency, testing, to alter the order and progress of children. *Pygmalion in the Classroom* was the title of his book, words that made us old progressive education graduates recall that fateful and yet hopeful word, "potential." "Tommy has the potential . . . " was written in every letter my school sent home. I hated the sound of it, but in time the idea that a number of physical, cognitive, and emotional capabilities were under my own control, were present, in other words, in my blood and muscles, was helpful, life-giving even.

This is the feeling millions of children will never know, precisely because it has been *proven* to them that they haven't got what it takes.

Perhaps it was genetically determined, and they should rush home and scold their parents, perhaps it wasn't but either way, they are, at age ten, finished. The remainder of grammar school and high school is predetermined. They will go out exactly as they went in, only several inches taller. This is the custodial ethic that overrides so many schools. No matter what its variations, the *proof* of its viability is the intelligence and psychological test. "I'm sorry, Tom, I can't weave straw into gold. You've seen his scores. You know what the kid's problem is."

For years schools have divided students into so-called ability groupings. In the beginning those making the divisions might have been a little insensitive, and so the names they selected for their groups hurt some people. College-bound students met in one room, the emotionally and mentally retarded met in another. Later, to lessen the pains and self-consciousness of this stratification procedure, psychologically sophisticated staff members divided children into the redbirds and the bluebirds, the oaks and the elms, or the deers and the crocodiles. But it rarely made much difference. A certain group of students claimed they didn't know what their new name meant, but other groups knew exactly what bluebirds or crocodiles signified: They were being labeled dummies! Dummies without recourse, moveover, because assignments were based on test results and the assessments of well-trained educators. And so, like students in the so-called underdeveloped nation described above, many American schoolchildren had their entire educational destinies established by the time they were ten. For in the stratifying of these children, getting out of one track into a higher one seemed in many schools to be a most difficult, if not impossible, task. Schools, these children learned quickly, were microcosms of society, the real world in miniature, and the lack of mobility in the tracking system might well be a valuable learning experience of what they would face when they graduated, if they did graduate.

For years the academic as well as political aspects of tracking went unchallenged, although it is not true that the students and their parents were ignorant of the various features of tracking. On the contrary. Everyone knew full well what the test scores and the eventual groupings meant. The lack of challenge was due to the fact that open political attack on education was not yet a legitimate action, and so people waited. Now, as sufficient numbers of people recognize the political evils of tracking, and the anachronistic theories of education that for so long underwrote it, the placement of students into so-called ability groups has become a legal and civil rights issue, as well as questionable educational policy. Again and again it turns out that tracking is used for the oppression of certain young people almost in the same way that cities and governments manage to keep certain people penned together in a clearly demarcated geography.

If there is one point to remember from this discussion, it is this: Classification of students by testing will inevitably reflect existing political and cultural realities. Whatever test we use to diagnose the capabilities of children, these tests will be biased. Sometimes, in a humanitarian mood, we disregard the tests and merely work especially hard with those students who seem to need extra help. But sometimes, whether intentionally or unwittingly, we classify certain students as being incompetent, retarded, slow, uneducable, and proceed to use these classifications as justification for the inferior treatment we show them and their families. Naomi Feigelson Chase makes a similar point most powerfully in her book on child abuse, *A Child Is Being Beaten*. If we can prove that poor families, and especially minority families, physically abuse their children more than affluent white families, we have therefore justified our not supporting these poor families and our taking their children away from them.

If we need evidence of racial discrimination in misclassification we need only examine the disproportionate numbers of minority children assigned to special education classes within their schools. The Children's Defense Fund studied 505 school districts in Arkansas, Georgia, Mississippi, and South Carolina that had reported their special education information to the government's Office of Child Research. All 505 districts had students enrolled in classes for the so-called emotionally and mentally retarded. Here are some of the Children's Defense Fund's findings: Over 80 percent of the students in these emotionally and mentally retarded classes were black, but only 40 percent of the total enrollments of these districts was black. Forty-six percent of the districts indicated that 5 percent or more of their black children were in classes for the emotionally and mentally retarded, but less than 1 percent of these districts reported the same percentage of white children in their special classes. The chance of being in a special class for emotionally and mentally retarded students was five times greater if one were black than if one were white. In fifty of the districts the chances were ten to one.

Information of this type on northern districts follows the same pattern. In Davenport, Iowa, again according to the data compiled by OCR, 22 percent of public school students enrolled in classes for the emotionally and mentally retarded were black. Yet less than 7 percent of the total student enrollment in these schools was black. In Davenport, Denver, and New Bedford, Massachusetts, the chance of a black child being assigned to a special class was about three times greater than for a white child. And let us recall this is information compiled by the government, based on the reports of school districts. The picture may even be worse.

For the majority of students assigned to special classes the conditions are sure to be worse. While special classes in some American schools are the place where truly exceptional learning takes place, the typical class of this kind often represents little more than a cell where children are sequestered within their own schools. It is as if the children are already being excluded from school. Indeed, special education classes, particularly for poor and minority children, may represent the first step of their leaving school, often forever.

We must remember that classification is part of a political and economic, as well as educational, process. The evaluations of children are at best subjective. Many children, diagnosed as mentally retarded, are never even given medical examinations. Still, schools receive funds for program aid to help them serve the emotionally and mentally retarded.

One last point. We do not yet possess adequate classifying techniques and strategies. The tests we continue to use are part of a multimillion-dollar educational industry, but they help us little in understanding human capacities and competence. Lest we believe the stereotype of so-called emotionally and mentally retarded children, we might keep in mind that all the children in the life studies in this chapter, with the exception of the boy called Ollie Taylor, have been "diagnosed" as emotionally or mentally retarded. The words of a gentle educator Judah L. Schwartz must not be forgotten: The information yielded by tests indicate only that a child *didn't* do something or say something. The information never indicates that a child *can't* do something or say something. Add the test bias to the variability of the scores due to the environment in which the test is administered and the personality, behavior, and physical characteristics of the tester, and one has a picture of the status of most so-called intelligence and capability tests. It is a picture that comes more into focus through the words of a child who has just learned that his test scores have earned him a place in the lowest academic track of his inadequate grammar school:

"They told me in school that I'm stupid. I didn't know what they were talking about but they just kept saying it. Told me there was no use talking back to them because they had it in their tests, everything they wanted to know about me. I said I should be in the other group, because those kids were learning more and besides, they were getting all the best teachers in their classes. I didn't want them to put me in the class which they put me in. But they said it was what they *wanted* to do, it was what they *had* to do 'cause they don't decide what classes to put the student in, the tests decide that for them. People don't decide.

"I was thinking that maybe I should take a rest from school because if they're putting me in that worst class then I don't see any reason why I should be there at all. When you're in that class they don't even care if you go to school or not. All they care about is that their records are right. They got me tested the way I'm supposed to, 'cause you can't refuse it, you got to be tested if they say so. So now I'm tested. So now they know. They think I'm stupid. If they don't think so then all they have to do is go into that office and look inside my folder and then they can see. 'We know you're a real smart guy,' they'd say, 'but the test knows better. We test everybody, and you're dumber than everybody except for all the nobodies we're putting in the same class with you.'

"I think you should be able to tell them whether you want to take those tests. Maybe if I said no way man, no way I'm going to answer any of your questions except the ones my teacher asks, maybe I could go and be with those other kids in the better class. I saw them testing one girl yesterday. They asked her politely, and she went with them. I followed them. You know why they were testing her? Because she talked too smart to be in the same class with the rest of us. She did talk smart too. I was thinking she was real smart, smarter than me.

"They tested her 'cause they *wanted* to get her out of that class. That's why they did it. They wanted her to get out of there with us. But they don't want that with me. They don't want to teach me nothing at that school. They don't want me to get smarter 'cause if I get too smart they'll have to put me in a higher group like they did with that girl. They ain't helping me to read better or faster. All they do is keep testing me to see if I'm doing things any better. But how can anyone get smarter if nobody's teaching 'em nothing. How'm I suppose to read faster and then remember everything I'm reading too if everybody's running around testing everybody. Teachers are supposed to teach, not test! If they spent their time teaching they wouldn't have to test us all the time. Even if they don't teach us they could spend more time with us so if somebody asked them is that kid smart, they'd know. They'd know even without testing."

Just about everyone living in the apartment building on the corner of Clayborn and South Plaine calls Audon Moses "Big Mo." Her grandson, Cornell Greenwood, who is thirteen, maintains a special relationship with her; he gets to call her, "Biggest Mo." Audon loves the name; she loves Cornell, too, and her six other grandchildren, but even their busy activity around the small apartment or their parents' easy style does not seem to heighten the energy in her body. Approaching seventy, she is barely able to move about and take care of herself anymore.

"Just getting my one foot and then the other off of that mattress every morning is enough exercise for me," she has told me. "Takes all the little bit of strength I've got to drag that big right leg over that ugly blanket and drop it on the floor. I'll be lying there, you know, watching my leg, cheering for it to get the hell off that bed. Probably do best to get one of those children who's always running around here to get it off of there for me. Feeling tired too. Always feeling tired now, like I had this invisible sickness creeping all around inside me. Takes me fifteen minutes to get my two legs off that bed. And then, when I do, all that happens is they touch that cold floor, and I'm thinking maybe I better get them back up on the bed for a little while, you know. But hell, takes too much energy to get 'em both back in the bed when I've just gone and spent all that time trying to get 'em on the floor first try. More likely I swing that big right one over the top and drop it right in the ash tray I got down there near the side of the bed. Can't move it right away when I ought to, 'cause I'd have to get out of bed to do that. I can't see it either. So like I say, I'll drop it over the bed there and smack it right down into that fancy ash tray my son gave me."

Audon Moses loves to hear her grandchildren laugh, and when she realized that I too was part of her audience, it only encouraged her. In the five years that I've known her there has never been a visit without at least one good laugh.

"I love to see a man like you who looks so worried most of the time show the world those nice teeth of yours. Go on, smile for Big Mo. Tell her what you're writing. What's the new book going to have in it?"

"Probably stuff about intelligence tests and the business of students being put in tracks," I answered, almost hoping she would help me with my work. My words stopped any playfulness she might have had in mind.

"Well now, you've cut quite a piece out for yourself this time, ain't you? Better talk to the children about that. All I know about that is what they tell me, coming home every day with their stories and their homework and their grades. Far as I can tell they're all born smart, it's just that they don't work hard enough. Maybe some of the teachers don't push 'em to work hard enough either. Maybe they let 'em get away with too much. You ain't got a thing to brag about in the world until you've got an education. You hear this child or that one saying how she's so pretty. 'Look at me Big Mo, ain't I pretty?' That don't mean nothing. I'd tell her too. Right to her face. 'Child, Big Mo thinks you may be the prettiest little girl in the world, next to Big Mo herself, but don't you come back until you can show me how *smart* you are.'" She whispered the word smart as though it were a term of sacredness. "'You come back here someday to Big Mo and you say, 'Big Mo, I have got to be one of the smartest, best-educated, intelligent people walking around on this here land.' 'Then you got something child. You've got the best the world can offer. This world anyway. Don't you get yourself involved with anybody but the right somebody, and don't you work on anything but what your teachers say you should be working on. Then you come on back to Big Mo and tell her how you've learned all these things. You tell her you've got great plans, plans that include getting more education. Maybe by then old Mrs. Moses here will be able to get both her heavy old feet off this stinking mattress.'"

"Biggest Mo," Cornell Greenwood said one day after I had been visiting with his grandmother, "she's all right for an old lady."

"She sure thinks well of you."

"Yeah," he said showing his modesty. "She thinks all her family is real special and stuff."

"She's got her ideas about school too, doesn't she?" I smiled.

"She don't know about school," Cornell replied angrily. He had been leaning against a wall in the Greenwood living room, but now he pushed himself away from it and took a step back from where I was sitting. "She thinks all you have to do is work hard, obey the teachers and you'll get smart. She doesn't know. She's never been to my school. It ain't anywhere near like what she thinks. Like, you could be the smartest person in the school but if you're black they won't put you in the good classes, unless maybe if you're a super athlete. Then they give you some advantage but they think they're being nice. The rest of us, they give us the worst teachers, no matter how good we do. They keep telling us if we work hard they'll advance us into a different division, you know, but they never do. They'll help the athletes and some of the real good-looking kids, 'cause they like them, they show 'em off. I'm as smart as anybody in that school but you'll see, they'll fix it so I don't go to college. They always have their ways of stopping me. You'll see how they'll do it."

"IQ tests?" I asked cautiously.

"Yeah, that's one way."

"How does that work, Cornell?"

"Well, say they want you to stay where you are, they give you an IQ test and say you did bad. You can't argue to no one. The dude says 95, you got 95. Or like, if they want you out of their class, they'll put you in some special ed class. What do they care? We got kids in our school, they've been in those special ed classes all their lives! Every year they keep going back to those classes and there's nothing in the world wrong with them. We ask the teachers, 'Hey, what they got him in there for? What'd he do?' 'Oh, he did bad things,' they'll say. Or they'll say, 'Old Jonah he's a *strange* little boy. Something wrong with his brain. Been that way since he was a little tiny baby. He can't learn the right way like the rest of us. And that's a fact!' But that's a lot of stuff, man, 'cause we'll know different. Old Jonah see, he's got a brother or sister maybe, and they know there's nothing wrong with him. Folks at school just don't like him, that's all. So they shut him up in that special ed class. Teachers try to tell us kids like him will turn better in there but we know it's a prison. I don't care what they lie to us, because we always got ways of finding out the truth. But I'll go pitch a bitch when one of those high and mighties goes around thinking I don't know what the truth is."

Cornell was steaming mad. Audon always quieted him down when he got like this, at least she did in front of me. I suspect she did the same when I was gone. She would throw in a few words too about behaving politely in front of company, while Cornell, who was already uneasy about talking to a white visitor in his home, would give her a look as if to say, I'm no child anymore. You take care of the little children and I'll take care of myself. But Audon, I could see, valued Cornell's outrage. She knew he "had it," as she said. He wouldn't "let things go on as they had all these years." Cornell and his friends will change things no matter what it takes, because they keep their eyes and ears open and know when to do the same thing with their mouths. And that's a sign that they're intelligent. It doesn't matter, see, how people answer somebody else's question. Even a teacher's. What matters is that children like Cornell and his friends understand what it's like living in the real world. They know what's happening to them at the school. They know everything there is to know about what's going on. The secrets have been told. They used to have a kind of a sheet they'd throw on themselves and all their institutions," Audon said, "especially where black folks were involved. But this generation, with the help of their elders, have pulled that sheet away, and there's America, the rich and the poor, the black and the white, just laying out there naked like a woman ready for her lover to come in that front door of hers, for everyone to see. But these kids see it all in a special way. They see it and behind it too. Every last one of them. 'Cause they got it. The intelligence I mean."

Cornell was looking around the room, wanting to say something else, about school presumably, but checking to make certain Audon wasn't able to hear him.

"I think she's asleep," I said, trying to encourage him to speak.

"She don't let me say my piece."

"I think she would."

"You don't know her," he protested.

"Not as well as you, but I have a sense of what she believes and what she stands for."

"I tried to tell her about the way they run their intelligence tests at the school and she didn't believe it. She told me I made it all up."

"Tell me, Cornell. What stories?"

"You won't believe them either."

"Try me. I've got some stories myself."

He was clearly interested. "Oh, yeah? What you got?"

"Kids given IQ scores without ever being given IQ tests."

"Right on! I'll tell you something else. We got a boy in our school took one of them tests and scored seventy—something. Everybody knows he ain't that dumb. Teacher, she was surprised to find that out too, so she asked him how come he did so bad? He told her it was because partly he got so scared he couldn't think straight and partly 'cause when he'd take too much time or miss something, the man giving the test would say, 'Well, if you don't know that one and it's the easiest, no sense giving you the rest?' Then another kid, he said that when he took the test the man kept telling him he was sounding like he wasn't only dumb but sick in his mind, you know. He kept saying, 'Maybe, we better stop, maybe we better stop.' So finally the kid got so frightened, they stopped and he wasn't half way through the test. But then they put down his score without anybody saying he'd only worked half the test. Everybody's got a story like that, man. Everybody.

"You know my sister Paula? She was taking the test and they came to the part where they got these blocks, you know, and you're supposed to match up the design on these little cards. So she starts working on the first one, and the guidance counselor, Mr. Kiplinger, he's sitting there real stitch ass, you know, like he really knew his business, timing her with this big stop watch. So Paula's working away, looking at her blocks, then looking back at the little cards." Suddenly, Cornell began to laugh out loud. Nothing he did could suppress his laughter. "She's working there, see," he continued, trying to catch his breath and looking over his shoulder for fear that Audon might have heard him, "putting all these blocks together, only she figures out there's two blocks missing. Well, she's ready to lay her bitch on him when he says, 'Smile awhile, Pretty Paula Face. You go on and do the best you can with the two blocks missing. Don't make no difference. Just go on like they were there.' So she does. Each time she finishes a design she says, 'There it is, and the other two blocks would go, like, here and there,' you know." Cornell poked twice in the air as if pointing to the missing blocks. "So old stitch ass he smiles and compliments her, but all the time he's marking on the page that she couldn't figure it out. She could see what he was writing all the time. That's why her score was low, and why she stayed in the same class.

"I don't know this one boy, but Derond Williamson told me about a kid who did real well on his test. Fact he did so well that when he got done the woman giving him the test stuck out her hand, you know, to shake his hand. So he just walked away. Spun around, man, dug that heel of his into the rug and departed. So she yells at him, 'Where you going, boy? I'm waiting here to shake your hand.' 'You ain't touching my hand,' he goes. 'Oh yes I am,' she goes. He goes, 'I don't know of a single rule in the Constitution of the United States that says I got to shake your hand!' 'Don't you give me stuff about the Constitution. In this school you'll do as I say!' 'I did your little whitey test,' he goes. That's what he said. 'And that's all I was supposed to do. Nobody told me about shaking no lady's hand at the end.' Now she's really screaming at him but he don't pay her no mind at all. He just goes. So she takes a whole lot of points away from him, and they put him in that special ed class I was telling you about. That kid was three years older than me. He was sixteen and a whole lot smarter. He just proved that on the woman's own test, but he committed the fatal sin, man. He misbehaved. He talked back to the goddess. But nobody ever said nothing about her calling him boy. He was in that class half the year, before they sprung him. Then they put him in the second year class, where everybody was too young for him. I tell you, man, that dude, he was really smart. I heard him talk. He could find a word for everything, man."

"He finish school?" I wondered.

"Not a chance. He left school two weeks after they sprung him from special ed. I saw him hanging around outside a couple of times after that, but he's gone now. Maybe he's in the army." His voice had become soft. "Maybe the streets got him."

Cornell stared at me without speaking. Then he sighed deeply, and his eyes closed half way as though he could see Paula, frustrated by the absence of the two small wooden blocks. This time he didn't smile. "Hey mama," he whispered, "look what they've done to my score. They do it to us everytime. Move us here, move us there, pushing us around all the time. It ain't what school's supposed to be. You know what you got to learn in that school, in all these schools? You got to learn where your place is. If they think you're dumb, they put you in that special ed class until you drop out of school, which is what they want you to do. If you got too many brains showing they paint over your test scores so no one will come around and ask, how come this kid ain't in a high division? Up and down, we're a bunch of yo-yo's. If anybody'd ever stop to think what we got to do to finish they'd know where we're spending all our energy. Hell, getting out of bed ain't no easier for me than for my grandmother. What do I got to get out of bed for? What do they think I'm supposed to be doing in school that matters? I ain't learning from school, I'm learning *about* that school. They're teaching away, but I see way behind their sweet asses. You want to have a fair intelligence test, you ask those kids, tell me which three teachers in this school can you trust, and prove it! I wouldn't even ask 'em about the principals. Or you could ask, name twenty different things about racism and tell me who in the school practices each one of them. Or, tell me, the names of every black student in this school who went to college, and then write an essay telling how he made that little college trip when no one in the school gave him any help.

"They're all hung up in these IQ tests with the wrong things. They ain't honest tests. Everybody knows that. All the advantages go to the white kids. And since they mess all over with us, why do they even bother to take time to give us the tests? I'll tell you why. So's they can convince themselves that they're doing the right thing. So's they can sleep at night. Go on home to their old lady and tell her they did the best they could that day with those nasty little black boys and girls, that evil 11 percent. But those nasty little black boys and girls just couldn't do the tests, so they'll go into the special classes. Hate to do it to you little boys and girls, but you know the rules we've written here for you all. Doing the best we can." Cornell's imitation had ended.

"Hell, that Kiplinger was probably spreading his fat stitch ass over Paula's blocks so to make sure she'd flunk. He got a glimpse pretty quick how smart she is and he knew there'd be no way of keeping her back after that. Folks like they got there would eat those blocks 'fore they'd be honest enough to admit black kids got what it takes to be intelligent.

"They control us with those tests, man. They got us dancing on the end of those scores. Hey mama," he shouted out, looking upward, "they're going to break my ass just like they broke my score. 'I ain't going to give you no trouble, teach,'" he announced to an imaginary person. "'I won't try to bust out of my division. Just let me take the good courses. Let me see if I can do 'em. Let me show you what I know. You folks got to change your minds about this intelligence idea. You got to learn from us and *our* intelligence. You think, lady, we could make it this far without being super intelligent? You think we don't know what's happening? You think we're blind and stupid? You bet your fat ass, lady, I ain't going to shake your hand. I'll let the streets get me too 'fore I stoop to you! You going to tell me that the guy who invented the divisions and prisons we got in the school was intelligent? You ever hear those people talking, lady? They ain't intelligent. They're dumb, man. I mean, where they're supposed to have brains they got fuzz. Golden white fuzz.'" Cornell was grinning. His eyes met mine.

"What are you thinking?" I asked.

"I was just thinking that when I go to decide who's the most intelligent person in the world, it comes out to be my grandmother. She's got wisdom, man. She's wise, man. She knows about things she's never even seen. She ain't never once been near my school, and she knows it. Hell, she ain't even ever been to school that anyone can remember. Least she says she ain't. But she knows. Grant the lady her due. She knows what a kid needs to know. She says her heart tells her more than her brain, that's why she knows she's smart."

I remembered Audon using the same phrase with me once, only she had said, "A person who knows when to listen to his heart and not his brain is bound to be a wise person."

"She's smart, all right," Cornell was saying. "She's the reason I stay on. I ain't going to drop out and let her down. Even after she dies I'll keep at it, no matter what they do to me at school. Paula says we got some of Biggest Mo's blood, which is all right. You can bet I'll be plenty careful not to cut myself so I won't waste a drop. I'll say okay if I end up like her, even laying in that bed. I'd be like that, 'cause her brain is going every minute; it's going and she's learning something about life, something that if she can't use she passes on to us. They may be shrinking us to death in school, but my grandmother's making us big."

"You've got a grandson that sure admires you," I told Audon later that same week.

"I've got all good grandchiljen," she replied. "I hate to hear how the schools hurt them. Been going on too long, seems to me. No sense to it anymore. What's anybody got to prove by it now? No sense hurting children. Not just my children, but all these children, sending them out where they'll only find trouble. Everybody can see that. Oh, what the hell." Audon's mood had changed suddenly as it so often did. "If I could get my old body out of this house I'd probably go with those children and make a little trouble myself. I'd like to hear the sounds out there. Haven't been outside, you know, in eleven years. All I got is the television and a few books, and the words those children and their parents got for me. Eating ain't too exciting. News just gets me mad, but it don't teach a person much. I depend on those kids now for feeding me whatever food they got left over from living. And what I hear is that their school is closing off more things to them than it is opening things for them. They don't let them advance, don't treat 'em fair, and they sure got their ways to stick 'em. Miracle of it all is that they stay intelligent about so many things; who they are, where they come from, where they might like to be going. There's no way to measure that sort of thing, you know, not with all the tests in the world. Only person can measure thw is the Man who gave it to them." Audon was leaning her weight to one side of the bed, straining to see where the ash tray was. The room was dark and very cold. Finally she gave up and lay back, flicking the ashes of her cigarette on the floor. "The Lord makes them smart, then their parents got the problem of keeping them that way, which ain't as easy as you might think when you stop to consider what everybody does to them, or might like to do."

There is a boy named B.J. Harris. He is a black boy, ten years old. He lives with his parents, two brothers, and four sisters. His father works in the shipping room of a firm that makes musical instruments. His mother, whose employment is limited because she has her own children to care for, works parttime as a cleaning lady and baby sitter. There are three children younger than B.J.

Small, frail-looking, a boy of few expressions, B.J. Harris has done his school work as diligently as he could, but usually with minimal success. "He tries," his mother says, looking up toward the ceiling as if to make certain God too has heard her. "I see the way he's worked, I know he tries. But it's never enough. If they paid a little more attention to him, maybe that would help. I think maybe it would too, you know. B.J. never has a problem passing his subjects, it's when he thinks he could do better than all right that things start coming down on his head. You take last year. There never was the slightest complaint from his teachers. I used to go there and talk with them and they'd always say he was doing fine. Not excellent, you understand, just fine. That was good enough for his father and me, you know what I mean? We knew he wasn't a genius like his sister Doreen. All we wanted was for him to pass on to the next grade and make sure no one put him in with the serious problem children. They got retarded children in the school, children who don't learn so fast as the others. No problem, no problem, the teachers told us. We'd always smile, you know. Just as long as he was keeping up with the other children. Didn't want him to repeat any time, that's all we were praying for, you understand.

"So, the year finished up, and we were told he did good enough to pass. They weren't saying fine this time, just good enough to pass. I was a little surprised. I could tell they were holding something back that last meeting. Mr. Harris wasn't with me that night. I went down with my sister, and we could see that B.J.'s teacher was keeping something from us. I thought maybe they were going to hold him back, but nobody said a word. I figured B.J. made it by the skin of his teeth.

"This September he goes to school and everything's all right for a week, two weeks maybe. Boy comes home from school looking all right—he's never one to let you know how he's feeling, like his father in that way—and I don't worry about anything. All I think about is that he did it. Then one day he comes home and says he ain't going to be with his friends anymore, in the same class. 'You flunk?' I asked him. I mean, I was surprised 'cause I had went to the school, and they said everything was all set for the next year. B.J. said he didn't flunk. Exactly. That's what he said, 'exactly.' 'What'd you do?' I asked him. I figured he made trouble. 'They got me in a special class,' he says. 'What kind of special class?' I ask him. 'I don't know,' he says. 'Just a special class with different kids.' 'They got you in the fourth grade, B.J.?' I ask him. 'I think so,' he says. 'I think it's the fourth grade.' 'What do you mean you *think* it's the fourth grade? Don't you know what grade you're in?' I knew, see, that he wasn't about to be moving up an extra grade. 'You go back there tomorrow" I told him, 'and you ask those people what grade you're in. I don't understand how a child can be in school and he don't even know what grade he's in. You do that for me, B.J.!'

"So he goes to school the next day and asks the teacher. I didn't go to work that day so I was waiting for him, sitting outside talking, waiting for him to come home and tell me. He comes up to me where I'm sitting in the sun, and we don't even say hello. He just says, 'It ain't the fourth grade or the third grade. It's a special grade.' At first I thought he didn't know what he was talking about. 'You got to be in one grade or the other,' I told him. I remember shouting at him out there. We couldn't figure it out. Mr. Harris and I were getting ready to go to the school and find out for ourselves, 'cept you hate to go there all the time 'cause it makes the boy think you don't believe him.

"Then I understood. They got him in the special class with the problem children. That's what the boy was trying to tell me. He didn't want to come right out and say special class, 'cause he was disappointed and beginning to feel real bad. You can understand that. I understood. Women I was sitting with they understood too. But I felt ashamed. Something was wrong with the boy, and we never knew it. I thought everybody would think we were hiding his problem, making believe he could go to the same school with everyone else. But like I say, when school was out last year I went there and asked the teachers and they said everything was fine. 'You're sure now?' I said. They were sure. So that's where he is. They got him in their special class. They say if he does well maybe they can put him back where he belongs, with his friends, you know, in the real fourth grade."

That indeed was where B.J. Harris was, in one of the school's special classes for the emotionally and mentally retarded, the children with learning disabilities. Diagnosed and tested, the twenty-eight children in B.J. Harris's "new" class seemed happy enough when I visited them. They were, I imagined, having a better time in school than most of the students I knew in the third, fourth, and fifth grades. They were not what one normally thinks of as emotionally and mentally retarded, the type one sees in special schools and institutions, but one always exaggerates the severity of the problem and the personality traits associated with this predicament.

Don't let yourself overromanticize these children, any children, I warn myself repeatedly. And especially not B.J. Harris, just because his parents are articulate and his brothers and sisters such exceptional youngsters. You can hate the tests, and all that they mean, but somebody somewhere "studied" this boy and test results are test results. Compassion and utopian philosophies of education cannot break a system that depends so heavily on numbers, psychological pronouncements, and technology. There comes a time when one must accept medical and paramedical diagnoses and procedures. B.J. Harris was in his special class, not overly happy about his situation but going to school every day and probably not thinking about his own destiny as much as I was. His parents had made their peace with the school's decision, and the year would now flow smoothly again.

After two months in his special class, however, B.J. Harris had stopped going to school. The class was tiring him, which was his word for boring him, and causing him to feel anxious. Each day there was less and less for him to do. Several children in the class, he reported, felt the same way. They would do some reading with a teacher, but then she would have to attend to the others for whom the written word meant little. It was days before they resumed work together. B.J. found himself killing time, sitting in the same corner of the room watching the teacher and the other children. Most upsetting, he began to believe that school was making him act like the other children in the class who he knew were far worse off than he. His belief was only confirmed by the reactions to him of his friends in the regular classes. After all, if he had been put in a special class, there must be something wrong with him. Trying to account for the change in B.J.'s status, they might have thought that he was a little weird to begin with.

B.J. was never able to verbalize the thought that the special class would cause him to become retarded, but I knew that he sensed this as a possibility. He sensed it the same way he sensed the illogicality of his own thinking on the subject. He was not as good as the others, so the school removed him from his regular class. Still, it didn't figure that by simply switching classes he had now become irregular.

The perplexing thing to me was that B.J. seemed brighter in December, weeks since he had last attended school, than ever before. Not only that, he seemed as intelligent as any of the children I knew in his regular class. I strenuously disagreed with his assessment that the special class was harming him, although I knew only too well that in theory he was right. The harm those classes might do to children who don't belong in them, I told his mother, was not showing. Mrs. Harris seemed pleased to hear it. She too was worried about the effect of the experience on B.J., especially since no one could tell her that next year would see him back in the regular fourth grade. Like me, she and her husband were concerned about what the special class and B.J.'s extended absence meant for his future in the school and after that as well.

"I think he's just as smart as he was," she said one afternoon shortly before Christmas.

"I think he's very smart, Mrs. Harris, and with your permission I'm going to do a little investigating."

"You got it," she said quickly.

A friend in the registrar's office let me see B.J. Harris's official school folder. The test results were utterly surprising. His aptitude and IQ scores were far lower than I would have predicted. As much as one wishes school procedures and facilities were different, the placement of this boy in a special class seemed absolutely appropriate. In a minute the numbers had convinced me too. The only remaining thorn was the lack of coincidence between my subjective assessments and the so-called objective rankings revealed by the tests. Sadly, my first impulse was to derogate my impressions. You can carry this personalized rating only so far, I mumbled to myself in the small records office. Perhaps I should pull the records of some other kids to see how far off my impressions were of their intelligence too.

"Get what you want?" the registrar's assistant asked when I returned the folder to her.

"Not at all."

"Something missing from his records?"

"No, no. The stuff's all there. I just hate thinking someone's so special or clever and seeing his test results . . ."

" . . . and he's not that smart," she finished the sentence for me.

I telephoned Mrs. Harris and advised her of B.J.'s test scores. My words about impressions not coinciding with numbers must have sounded hollow and patronizing. No one needed to tell her that her son was not retarded or emotionally disturbed. "Can I come over this afternoon and talk to B.J.?"

"What about?"

"I don't know. The tests."

"Why not." I heard her disappointment and resentment. She had been hoping that something might have turned up. The matter was beginning to sound like a detective story. B.J. had committed a crime and was being held by the police. All the evidence pointed to his guilt, and only his parents and me believed in his innocence. I thought of sneaking out his folder and changing the numbers. "Hey look," I would call out, "they made a mistake. B.J.'s IQ. isn't 85. It's 185! Put him back in the regular fourth grade, in the fifth grade, maybe." "Thank God for you, Tom," the registrar's assistant would sigh. "You've saved him." Except that she, along with many teachers, had already seen B.J.'s folder. Everybody doublechecks these things.

"B.J.," I said to him when we were settled in the living room of the Harris apartment, "tell me about the tests you took." The boy looked over his shoulder toward the kitchen where his mother was sitting. She had purposely left us alone.

"Do you remember taking a test last year?"

He nodded yes.

"How long did it last? Can you remember that?"

His face was blank.

"About an hour, something like that?"

B.J. nodded again and looked about the room. He could not have been more uncomfortable. Why I was forcing him to recall this ordeal I'll never know.

"Okay, B.J. An hour. Okay?"

All he did was nod. I saw Mrs. Harris peek out behind the doorway. B.J. caught me looking at her and turned around.

"You talk to him," Mrs. Harris ordered her son. B.J. begrudgingly turned back to face me.

"All right. Did they ask you about words? What different words mean?"

He nodded.

"And give you sentences, tell you to do something with them?"

"Yeah," he whispered.

"Numbers too?"

"Hmm."

"They make you add and subtract?"

"Hmm."

"Multiply and divide? Stuff like that?"

He nodded.

"And blocks? They give you blocks to make designs with, you know?"

"Hmm."

"Little ones, some of them with red and white painted sides?" Unthinkingly, I was recalling items on the Wechsler *Adult* Intelligence Test.

B.J. continued nodding.

"Cartoons?" I grinned. "Little cartoons and you rearrange them to tell a story?"

"Hmm."

"Right?"

"Yeah."

"Oh, and situations where they ask you what you would do?"

He looked at me quizzically.

"'You know, like, what would you do if you found a letter on the sidewalk with a stamp on it?"

"Yeah." His answers were identical. Flat, dull, with maybe a touch of impatience mixed in. What was the sense of my grilling him? I imagined him wondering. Merely to prove to him that I was trained in psychological testing?

"Just a little bit more, B.J. All right?"

"Yeah." He wanted to see whether his mother was still in the kitchen, but he caught my stare and kept himself from turning around.

"B.J. this is important. Did they ask you questions about yourself after the test was over?"

He nodded.

"Like what your dad does, and how you think about things?"

"Yeah."

"Stuff like that, right?"

"Hmm."

"They ask you if you knew who the first President of the United States was?"

B.J. grinned to let me know he knew the answer to that one.

"Old George, " I smiled back.

"Yeah. George Washington."

"Hey, here's one, B.J. Do you know who was President before Nixon?" B.J.'s eye brows furled and his face was thrown into thought. Mrs. Harris leaned around the corner again. "It wasn't Kennedy," he was saying. "Johnson?"

"Absolutely. It was Johnson. Know his first name?"

"Ugh. Ugh."

"Remember it maybe?" I persisted. I'll give the boy my own IQ test, I thought. We can fudge the results and put him back in his old class.

B.J. was not embarrassed about not knowing President Johnson's first name. And then suddenly, as though someone had whispered it in his ear, he announced, "Lyndon."

"You've got it!" I shouted.

B.J. beamed with pleasure.

"You're smart, you know that?"

He smiled and nodded yes.

"You want to know something?" I began. "When I first asked you who was President before Nixon I didn't know the answer myself. I thought Kennedy for a minute there too."

B.J. hadn't stopped smiling. My words caused him to relax in his chair for the first time.

"I've been too tough on you, my friend. Let's quit."

B.J. said nothing. Mrs. Harris entered the living room. She too was smiling with pride. We were all acting as though a medical examination that had made us anxious was now completed, and the results were successful. She didn't ask, where do we go from here? For those few moments, we were relieved, happy even. I had automatically fallen into the pattern of an IQ tester, and they had both believed in my performance and in the assessments I now might make. I had done nothing but affirm the technology of testing and the fate it brought to this one child.

"One more thing," I called out to B.J. before leaving. "Do you by any chance remember the name of the person who gave you the test?"

He shook his head.

"Someone in the school though. I mean, you didn't leave the building to take it somewhere?"

First B.J. shook his head, then he nodded, then he looked at his mother and me with confusion.

I clarified my question. "In school?"

"Yeah. It was in school."

"A man give you the test?"

B.J. showed the same face he had when he had searched for President Johnson's first name. "Yeah, it was a man." He kept looking back and forth between his mother and me.

"Wasn't a woman?"

"I don't think so," he answered softly.

"Was it one of the teachers, B.J.?"

Again the puzzled look as if I were asking him to recall a dream.

"A teacher you know?"

B.J. was scratching his head, purposely accentuating a look of befuddlement.

"A guidance counselor probably," I came to his aid.

"Yeah. I guess so."

"Male guidance counselor. I ought to be able to find out who it was, Mrs. Harris. Maybe we can come up with something." The detective imagery returned. "B.J., you've helped a lot. Can you forgive me for being such a tough questioner? I really grilled you pretty bad."

B.J. smiled and looked away shyly, his mother's face shone with pride.

"I ain't quitting," I said. "I'm a pretty stubborn old man, you know." I stared at B.J. so he would know I was speaking to him. His expression told me that he understood what my efforts were all about. I would have given anything to tell him that everything was fixed and that he could return to his regular fourth-grade friends.

Other matters took me off the "Harris case" for a couple of weeks. It was the Christmas holiday anyway, and so I had to wait until school reopened in January. Finally, I went to the registrar's office and got the names of all the guidance counselors connected with the school. I contacted each person, not quite certain what I would ask if I discovered the person who had tested B.J. None of them had. One suggested that I telephone a man who had worked in the school last year but had subsequently moved to Arizona. Perhaps he had administered the test. At any rate, he was the only remaining possibility.

The man knew B.J. Harris quite well. Indeed B.J. was one of the last boys he had seen when he cleaned out his office at the end of June. He had never tested B.J., however, or anyone in B.J.'s class for that matter.

"What would you predict B.J.'s IQ to be?" I began timidly. "Or isn't that a fair question?" I hadn't yet told him that I couldn't locate the person who had administered B.J. the test.

"B.J. Harris?" He was thinking over my question. "I hate these estimations."

"It's probably foolish of me to ask."

"No, it's all right. Let's see. You know what his IQ is?" he wondered.

"Yes."

"Okay. Don't tell me. I'll take a shot at it. How's 105 hit you."

"Sounds good."

"That's right?"

"It says 85 on his sheet."

"Eighty-five?" The voice three thousand miles away had suddenly come alive. "Can't be."

"That's what it says."

"Who tested him?" he asked in a curious way.

"That's my problem. I don't know. No one here remembers testing him. I thought maybe you had."

"Never! On the bottom of the yellow sheet," he said excitedly, now caught up in my investigation, "there's a code number. Bottom right hand corner. The last three numbers are the tester. It's a six digit deal, I think. Something like that. But the last three will tell you. Does that nice woman still work in the office?"

"She does, yes."

"Get her to show you the card. She'll have a master chart of guidance counselors and teachers."

Our conversation went on a bit longer. I envied his location in the sun; he missed the snow, but mostly the students. He criticized the administration and school committee and hoped that someday there would be changes. It was better, he said, where he was now, but no one should think public education is a picnic anywhere. His kindness and thoughtfulness had reached easily across the country. His last words were greetings for B.J. and his friends.

The story of B.J. Harris's placement in a special class for children with severe learning disabilities may now be concluded. It is, as I have suggested, a case of grotesque manipulation of a human being.

There was, in fact, a code number at the bottom of B.J.'s test sheet. The last three digits of it, however, coincided with nothing at all. That is, they failed to correspond with the code number assigned to any teacher, counselor, or administrator. Moreover, as further interviewing and exploring showed that no one outside the school, as for example a hospital staff or welfare agency, had ever been consulted about B.J. Harris, it had to be concluded that he had been assigned an I score but that he had never been administered an IQ test! How this came about is a question that cannot be satisfactorily answered. Either a mistake had been made, or someone had purposely recorded test results in order to have this boy switched out of his regular class. Even after months of investigation a clear picture of exactly what happened does not emerge, and one is left to make inferences where it would be better to have facts.

Whatever occurred took place over the summer. That is clear, as Mrs. Harris herself was advised that B.J. had graduated from the third grade and was on his way to the fourth grade. By September, as we know, everything had changed. An assistant principal who had granted me permission to inspect the confidential school records of certain students left the school in October, after I had seen B.J.'s scores. My second trip to the record's office was made possible by his permission, although the school's principal was, naturally, upset by my investigation. I had incorrectly assumed that he knew of my arrangement with the now departed assistant principal. Almost every official in the school had access to these records, although students and parents do not. As an outsider with the explicit intention of attempting to find out what happened to B.J. Harris, I was always held in some suspicion by the school, but this is to be understood.

In any event the principal was shocked to learn of my discovery and at once attributed it to an unforgiveable bureaucratic error. He explained that the school tests all the children by the time they reach sixth grade, but that because of budgeting and time constraints, children in a particular class are not necessarily tested at the same time, or even in the same year. It is not surprising then, that B.J. might not have been tested while some of his classmates had been. The principal said, too, that guidance counselors and occasionally "special people" from outside the school were employed as testers. Their results then are transferred by staff members on to computer sheets and eventually filed by the registrar or her assistant. Because of the large quantity of forms and information constantly going in and out of students folders, it was impossible to tell just who put the actual test score on the sheet or placed the sheet in the folder. The safeguards are such, however, that getting information of any sort into a student's folder is hardly a difficult task. No one would have reason to check something like a code number on a testing sheet when filing it. That the code number was essentially a random number could be explained, again, as mechanical error just as easily as intentional cover up. And the fact that no one until the man in Arizona, a person thousands of miles away from the school, informed me of the code number can also be attributed to oversight. Surely the registrar's assistant would have reminded me of the number had she thought it an important piece in the puzzle.

Whatever was left to discover came through inquiries with teachers. It is no secret that most all schools have faculty groups that do not share ideologies and philosophies of education. Some people are openly critical of their school, even with a stranger like myself. Other people are undying supporters of the school; still others refuse to speak to outside investigators. And, as we know, teachers may be critical of one another, claiming their colleagues to be too permissive or too rigorous with students, too liberal or too conservative. Some teachers in B.J. Harris's school were shocked by the events of his case; others seemed less surprised. Some pointed at once to the fourth-grade teacher as a man "more than capable" of pulling off a stunt like faking IQ scores. Other teachers said the man was totally scrupulous and could never do such a thing. Some teachers confidentially accused certain guidance counselors of participating in the forgery. Other teachers believed that anyone accusing a guidance counselor of such an act should be immediately dismissed from the school. An event like this clearly draws the political lines of any school, but the conversations that take place produce very few real facts.

The major contradiction I uncovered involved the reports of B.J.'s own teachers. The third-grade teacher admitted telling the man who would have been his regular fourth-grade teacher that B.J., along with others in his class, was a "problem student," someone he should look out for. She was certain, moreover, that he belonged to a neighborhood pee-wee gang that had been committing muggings and purse snatchings. Although she could not prove it, she was convinced that B.J. carried a gun to school on several occasions. She said nothing, however, about the appropriateness of placing B.J. in a special class for children with learning disabilities. In contradiction, the fourth-grade teacher claimed that he made it a policy never to speak to other teachers about the students in his incoming class in order that he might form his own opinions of them. Presumably, then, he knew nothing about B.J. or the boy's alleged gang activities. As for the pee-wee gang, Mr. and Mrs. Harris had never heard of it and said it would be impossible for B.J. to participate in such an "awful group" without their knowing about it. B.J. himself laughed when I raised the allegation with him. But he was also insulted. "I don't carry a gun, man," he answered facetiously, "I bring in a tank. I'm surprised you ain't never seen it before." Although I believed him, I nonetheless checked out his denial with more than twenty students in the school who knew about the gang. Not one of them had the slightest doubt that B.J. was not involved. In fact many suggested he was too cowardly to be admitted by the pee-wees.

The evidence, such as it is, can hardly be said to prove conclusively that a manipulation of test scores took place. That this story is repeated many times in schools—and frequently involves black boys—indicates, however, that bureaucratic error is not the only explanation. Further investigation turned up eight more children in B.J.'s school who, because of "low IQ scores" had been taken out of their regular classes and placed in classes with so-called learning disability children. As was true in B.J.'s case, the code number of the tester of each of these children again coincided with no school personnel. All but one of this group were boys, all were black, in a school that is 18 percent black. Each of the children, the principal later told me, had been labeled "problem cases" by their teachers, but only one of them was doing poorly enough that he could be considered as having academic difficulty. In all instances, parents had followed their children's misfortunes closely, but no one had legitimate reasons for doubting the tests or questioning the children's reassignments.

In B.J. Harris's case, as in the case of three of the others with whom I spoke, the fright of school authority, and testing generally, was so great they actually were convinced they had taken an IQ test. My grilling of B.J., as well meaning as I hoped it would be, only reawakened his fright and his sense of having to be obedient to anyone connected with school. He nodded yes, therefore, to every question I asked. In retrospect, my inquiry about multiplication and division should have been a clue that he did not have the slightest idea what I was talking about. I never stopped to think that B.J. had not yet studied these mathematical techniques.

Ironically, to place the children back in their regular classes, IQ tests had to be administered to them. With their "new scores" properly recorded, all but one immediately returned to their normal homerooms. The single exception was a boy who the psychologist felt was "severely emotionally disturbed." (The psychologist, incidentally, was someone recommended by me. Wanting to settle the matter, the principal had generously accepted this recommendation for an impartial tester, a young psychologist who had been working in various school systems for several years. But by accepting him the principal was seen to be doubting the integrity of his own counselors, and his action had some unfavorable repercussions in the school.)

As for the acceptance of B.J. Harris by his regular fourth-grade teacher, little can be said. B.J. claims the man does not like him. The teacher claims it makes no difference to him who is assigned to his class. The students claim that the teacher never has publicly said anything about B.J.'s presence. He acts as if nothing had happened. So does the school which has never sent word in the form of explanation or apology to the Harris home.

Schools, no doubt, react in some fashion to the constant criticisms and investigations of them. Almost any sort of interviewing or prying will be met with resistance, if not open retaliation. Properly, teachers and administrators claim they have the right to work unencumbered, that an outsider like myself promotes even greater tension than the same investigation undertaken by someone associated with the school. One cannot help but be sensitive to this sentiment. The easiest thing in the world is to visit a school for a few days, criticize it, even with the best intentions, and move on, leaving teachers, administrators, and students exactly where they were. To serve in the role of investigator or ombudsperson—a role many school volunteers now play—threatens the very structure of the school and potentially the individual one is representing as well. As always, when improprieties are unearthed, the same old victims receive blame. It was not my intention to "go after" certain school personnel, to accuse them, or in any way threaten their employment or position in the school. Nor was it my intention to let the right of B.J. Harris to attend school in his regular class be violated. And, as is always true, there was a selfish motivation: For no matter how much I argued that testing was irrelevant or even destructive, I could not dismiss the discrepancy between his "tested" IQ score and my own assessment of his intelligence.

O llie Taylor is eleven years old. His family lives in Boston, and even though his father works fifty hours a week they are very poor. Ollie and his five brothers and sisters have all attended their neighborhood school, and all of them have ended up in the so-called bottom tracks. Failure to this boy is an inevitability. Almost every action he takes becomes a movement of extended time; always it ends in convincing him that he is, in his own words, worthless. And that feeling, I know from speaking with him for three years, can be traced directly to his school, not to his family where he receives encouragement and love and respect. His parents and grandparents tell me that the inner strength given him by God, and sustained by their enduring care for him, is going to be shattered by years of schooling and a tracking system that pounds into his head the notion that he is dumb, talentless, hopeless. And the assessments, he reminds me every time I see him, are based on scientific tests scored on computers. They cannot, in other words, be argued.

"I won't buy it," I told him one day after school, walking home from the ice cream store. "What about *me*, Ollie? Doesn't my assessment matter to you?" I asked immodestly. "I know a little something about children too."

"You know what, Tom?" he said, looking down at his ice cream as though it suddenly had lost its flavor, "nobody, not even you or my dad can fix things now. The only thing that matters in my life is school, and there they think I'm dumb and always will be. I'm starting to think they're right. Hell, I know they put all the black kids together in one group if they can, but that doesn't make any difference either. I'm still dumb. Even if I look around and know that I'm the smartest in my group, all that means is that I'm the smartest of the dumbest, so I haven't gotten anywhere at all, have I? I'm right where I always was. Every word those teachers tell me, even the ones I like most, I can hear in their voice that what they're really saying is, all right you dumb kids,

I'll make it as easy as I can, and if you don't get it then, then you'll never get it. Ever. That's what I hear every day, man. From every one of them. Even the other kids talk that way to me too."

"You mean the kids in the upper tracks?" I asked, barely able to hold back my feelings of outrage.

"Upper tracks? Man, when do you think I see *those* kids? I never see them. Why should I? Some of them don't even go to class in the same building with me. If I ever walked into one of their rooms they'd throw me out before the teacher even came in. They'd say I'd only be holding them back from their learning. I wouldn't go near them," he grumbled. "And they wouldn't come around us neither, I'm sure."

We crossed the street, and I had to grab his shoulder to keep him from walking in front of a bicyclist. He wasn't seeing anything except the insides of his school and perhaps, too, the visions that had been accumulating for so long in his mind.

"I'll tell you something else," he was saying, unaware of the ice cream that was melting on his hand. "I used to think, man, that even if I wasn't so smart, that I could talk in any class in that school, if I did my studying, I mean, and have everybody in that class, all the kids and the teacher too, think I was all right. Maybe better than all right too. You know what I mean?"

"That you were intelligent," I said softly.

"Right. That I was intelligent like they were. I used to think that all the time, man. Had myself convinced that whenever I had to stand up and give a little speech, you know, about something, that I'd just be able to go to it and do it." He tilted his head back and forth. "Just like that," he added excitedly.

"I'm sure you could too."

"I could have once, but not anymore."

"How do you know, Ollie?"

"I know."

"But how?" I persisted.

"Because last year just before they tested us and talked to us, you know, to see what we were like, I was in this one class and doing real good. As good as anybody else. Did everything they told me to do. Read what they said, wrote what they said, listened when they talked."

"How long was this?"

"Almost two weeks," he answered proudly, the ice cream continuing to fall over his hand. "Then they told me, like on a Friday, that today would be my last day in that class. That I should go to it today, you know, but that on Monday I had to switch to this other one. They just gave me a different room number, but I knew what they were doing. Like they were giving me one more day with the brains, and then I had to go to be with the dummies, where I was supposed to be. Like my vacation was over. So I went with the brains one more day, on that Friday like I said, in the afternoon. But the teacher didn't know I was moving, so she acted like I belonged there. Wasn't *her* fault. All the time I was just sitting there thinking this is the last day for me. This is the last time I'm ever going to learn anything, you know what I mean? Real learning."

He had not looked up at me even once since leaving the ice cream store. In fact I couldn't recall him having licked at the cone more than once or twice. "From now on," he was saying, "I knew I had to go back where they made me believe I belonged. I didn't even argue. I was just sitting there thinking I was like some prisoner, you know, who thought he was free. Like they let him out of jail and he was walking around, like you and me here, having a great old time. Then the warden meets him on the street and tells him they made a mistake and he has to go back to prison. That's what I was thinking of in that class.

"So then the teacher called on me, and this is how I know just how not smart I am. She called on me, like she always did, like she'd call on anybody, and she asked me a question. I knew the answer, 'cause I'd read it the night before in my book which I bought, and then my mother read the book to me too, after I'd already read it. So I began to speak, and suddenly I couldn't say nothing. Nothing, man. Not a word. Like my mind died in there. And everybody was looking at me, you know, like I was crazy or something. My heart was beating real fast. I knew the answer, man. And she was just waiting, and I couldn't say nothing. And you know what I did? I cried. I sat there and cried, man, 'cause I couldn't say nothing. That's how I know how smart I am. That's when I really learned at that school, how smart I was. I mean, how smart I *thought* I was. I had no business being there. Nobody smart's sitting in no class crying. That's the day I found out for real. That's the day that made me know for sure."

Ollie's voice had become so quiet and hoarse that I had to lean down to hear him. We were walking in silence, I was almost afraid to look at him. At last he turned toward me, and for the first time I saw the tears pouring from his eyes. His cheeks were bathed in them. Then he reached over and handed me his ice cream cone.

"I can't eat it now, man," he whispered. "I'll pay you back for it when I get some money."

4.

Dying a Different Sort of Death

Rituals, rules, and lack of rights underlie the history of poor and minority children in school. Actually, they underlie all children's educational experiences, but in the case of poor and minority children there is so much more that precedes the impact of any rule or missing opportunity. The prevention of life unfolding as it is naturally meant to do, the inhibition of any human action or pursuit is not always attributable to a piece of legislation, or, more likely, the absence of that legislation. An entire culture may impede personal growth and tamper seriously with the dynamics of human maturation.

It is not redundant to say that some poor children withdraw from school because they are poor, or black children because they are black. We have already examined the statistics that demonstrate these facts. Some children are too hungry in the morning to make their way to school. Others cannot keep up with schoolwork because the distance between their home and school is so great, and the means of transportation so inadequate or expensive. They are lucky to make it to school one or two days a week. There are children who work inside their homes as well as outside and who have no choice but to let their school attendance drop off. Even if they wanted to attend school, the infrequent buses from their communities to school mean that there is no way they can both do their chores and go to school. In the beginning they are able to keep up with schoolwork but slowly the capacity to handle all their responsibilities dwindles. The desire to be educated, however, does not decline, nor does their appreciation of school.

Unquestionably, the cost of transporting children to school may be an unbearable financial burden to some parents. Almost 20 million children, about 43 percent of all schoolchildren, are bused to school each day. (Less than 4 percent of this busing is for the purpose of racial desegregation.) In many states the cost of transportation runs to three dollars a week. While that may not sound like a great deal, this amount spread over time may actually mean dropping out of school for the child whose parents earn less than three thousands dollars a year.

Added to the transportation costs are various school fees. Many states may legally levy a school fee for such items as typing, science, and art courses, or they may charge for summer courses, which are required for some students if they are to remain in school. Textbook costs, too, may drive children out of school, though by law, most states must provide textbooks for their students. This does not prevent teachers from assigning additional books, which students must own if they are to pass their courses. In some Iowa school districts, schools rent students books at a cost. Colorado law requires that indigent students be given textbooks, but teachers determine whether a student qualifies as being indigent. From *Children Out of School in America:* "It is clear that whatever the policy is that makes free texts possible through specific request, it is ad hoc and not made public in the parts of the community that need it."

There is something else about poverty and institutional racism that makes schooling an especially difficult exlerience, and that is the toll they take on the human psyche and spirit. They cause one to be fatigued, to feel an extra pain, an extra embarrassment, shame. Many children not holding jobs, who have enough food and sleep well enough at night, cannot face the social aspect of school because they are ashamed of what we might call their "station in life" or injured by racist degradation. They dread being seen in the same shoes or dresses day after day, or they do not have proper shoes and clothing. They fear the moment in a social studies or English class when a well-meaning teacher may ask them to tell about their background, their parents and grandparents, their home and neighborhood. They have secrets to keep which they feel must never be divulged, particularly in school.

These children too may stop going to school. They would deprive themselves, it would seem, of their own rights to education. Their schools might deal with their shame or their being oppressed, if it could be gently brought out and honored. But possessing rights and having the amenities and opportunities to allow one to exercise those rights are two different things. For poor and minority children one of the many tragedies is that they cannot always reach the place where even the legislation that is behind them makes a difference.

Bobby O'Boy is the sixth of nine children. His father, who quit school at the age of twelve and worked parttime as a carpenter—parttime because jobs were scarce for a non-union man—died when he was forty from pulmonary emphysema. One of the older O'Boy children had graduated from high school by then; but two of the others dropped out soon after their father's death. Along with their mother, they urged their younger brothers and sisters to stay in school and graduate, but Mary O'Boy knew her youngest children were destined not to complete high school.

Bobby, who was almost ten when his father died, knew that he would follow in the path of his older brothers. The way was clear; like Jack and John O'Boy, who had lasted two years and then entered the army—even Freddy, who had made it into his fourth year before he left school—one stuck it out as long as possible, then quit. No one at the school seemed too concerned by the O'Boys dropping out, although several teachers had encouraged Freddy to keep at it for the last five months.

They used to say that when Bobby O'Boy was a kid of nine and ten, he was quite the basketball player. He would actually attract a small crowd of men when he played on one of the neighborhood's cracked black tar courts. Small for his age, he made up what he lacked in size by being a fighter and a backcourt general. He would pass the ball around to the bigger boys and hop about looking for the good play, an opening to the basket, his pale white skin flushed with red and his fine long blond hair bouncing in waves as he ran. Basketball was his world. At night he prayed that he would grow to be six feet six inches tall and become an all-scholastic player. Every year in the spring he taped up on his wall the pictures from the Sunday *Tribune* of the all-state players and circled their heights. Especially interesting to him was their year in school. One boy, Kevin Flaherty, became an instant hero to this ten-year-old when he was selected first-team all-state guard when only a sophomore. "That's the year to make it," Bobby told himself, "especially if you don't think you're going to finish high school. Make it first time around like Flaherty and get out clean."

The years following the death of Mr. John O'Boy were trying and difficult. The family did not talk much about him, but his absence was felt deeply. Bobby wished he could have his father back, even if it meant hearing him fighting and yelling when he was drunk or seeing the old man sitting in that sullen bitter way of his in front of the living room windows, going hours without saying a word to anyone. At least he was there. Mrs. Mary O'Boy, whose own formal education ended before she entered high school, took a parttime job as a cleaning woman in a hospital, as did sixteen-year-old Francine, one of the daughters. And so, with the two older boys working fulltime and still living at home, the family managed, although the strain of their precarious financial situation was taking a toll. The younger children were missing more and more days of school. They were sick more often after their father's death than ever before, and the duration of their illness was extended. That nobody was around to care for them didn't help any, but watching television was certainly more enjoyable than going to school.

From the sixth grade on Bobby O'Boy was always placed in one of his school's lower educational tracks. No one was surprised by this, least of all Bobby. Just talking with the other boys and girls convinced him that he was not as smart as they were, or so he continued to tell his family. Privately, he believed he could do as well as most of the other kids if the school ever gave him the chance. But it never did, and he never complained. One simply didn't complain about tracking. By the time he entered the large public high school a mile from his home, education for him had become a wasteful chore. He was learning next to nothing in the bottom tracks. All the teachers wanted of him and his classmates was to stay out of trouble. Their philosophy, however simple, perplexed him. At first the teachers refused his request to take interesting courses; then they changed their minds and let the lower-track students do anything they wanted, even if it meant drowning in the more difficult courses. It was as though in defiance they allowed students like Bobby to discover just how uninformed and unprepared they really were.

Throughout the grammar school and high school years, Bobby O'Boy felt himself slipping in some peculiar way he could barely describe. He was losing touch with most of the other students. Even the boys with whom he played basketball seemed to be growing distant from him. While he laughed a lot, surely as much as the others, and remained a popular young man, he couldn't help but feel sad most of the time in a way that made him think he might never again feel happy as he had as a child. Perhaps it was his father's death that troubled him, or watching his mother work as hard as she did and worry about whether there would be enough money. Nothing was working out well at all for the first-year high school student. If he had to prove himself worthy by comparing himself with retarded and brain-damaged children in a special education class, or with the basketball players in the neighborhood grammar school, he was slipping, or so Bobby O'Boy convinced himself.

The slipping ended in his sophomore year, when he was fourteen. On a Wednesday morning in March, Bobby got back three tests he had taken the previous week. He had flunked all three, and with incompletes in two courses from the prior term, poor grades in most all the other courses, and his already firm status in the bottom tracks, the idea of continuing school seemed futile. He left at the end of the day and never went back. The school telephoned the O'Boy home to inquire about him on that following Friday and several times again in the next week. Each time Bobby himself answered the calls and explained that he was ill but would be returning. At last the calls stopped, and Bobby O'Boy's formal education officially ended. The school never inquired about him again. Quite possibly, four years later, his file still remains in the drawer of active students.

Mary O'Boy used all her energy entreating her son to complete school. "Just finish this one year," she begged him, but Bobby refused. Already involved with some older boys who had dropped out, he was actively looking for work. "You need the money anyway, Ma," he argued gently with her. "I got guys who'll find me a job. I'm going to bring it home to you anyway, ain't I? So what's the fuss all about? I ain't moving out, am I? You don't see me packing my things or nothing, do you? I ain't running away from home, Ma. I'm going to make it better. I don't want you to work. That's all it is. You got a right to stay here, go out with your friends when you want to, have a little fun. I'll bet you ain't had a good laugh since he died. Right? I'm going to give you my salary and keep a little for myself. And you know what I'm going to do with the money I keep? You want to know?" Obligingly, Mary O'Boy nodded to her son. "I'm taking my girl to the movies and out to dinner. That's you, Ma!"

Mary O'Boy smiled. With her older sons about to enter military service and some of her younger children still in school, she knew that Bobby's point about money had merit. Still, he was a smart enough boy. He could have finished school. It must have been the older boys he had found, she reasoned, who got him to quit.

At eighteen, Bobby O'Boy, now out of school four years, works as a car mechanic at a small garage in downtown Boston. He has become a master mechanic for motorcycles. His co-workers say that in a few years he'll be able to fix anything in the country with wheels. He is pleased with the way his life is working out, although the old feeling of being distant from people remains. He does not, however, have the sensation of slipping the way he used to. Still, he thinks about his past and, of course, school.

"You want to know whether I think about the old days? Sure I do. I even think about going back one of these days, maybe trying to get my degree in one of these night school programs they got around here. I wouldn't advise nobody to drop out. Even if I make more money than the guy who finishes school, it's better to stay in and finish. Everybody knows I'm going to do better than the guy who finishes, unless he goes to college. Finishing high school and not going on don't mean nothing. I'm better off than that. Hell, I've been working almost three and a half years. That's a lot of money I've put away. And you don't think my Ma couldn't use some of that? Hell, she quit her job less than a year after I went to work. You better believe she was happy to see me working regularly. She'd have preferred me finishing at school, I know that, but with families like ours, you don't kid anybody about what you need the most. You need money. The big M. Just 'cause I stopped going to school don't mean, you know, that anybody stopped sending us bills.

"The life story of a kid like me is easy to tell. In the schools they got for us, you learn real soon whether you were born with brains. Once they put you in their tracks you know if you got 'em or not. I knew ten years ago I wasn't heading for nothing in school. You look around, you can see easy enough what happened to the guys who quit: A few of 'em got in some kind of trouble; most of 'em got jobs. Don't ask me how, but a lot of guys like me, not brainy up here," he poked at his head, "but good with their hands, they ended up with jobs. Not dynamite ones but good enough. So, for a couple of years, while I was faking my way in school, I got to know different guys who could help. I watched 'em all the time. Even played basketball with 'em. Charlie McInally and Sal Battaglia, Sally the Butcher they call him, were the guys I needed to get to know. So I got to know 'em. They're real good guys, you know. They did lousy in school just like me, but Salvatore, he got me my first job delivering at the pharmacy where he used to work, and then Charlie got me here.

"So I didn't suffer that much from quitting. Anyway, like I say, I may go back to school, I'm thinking about it, but I think about someday going into my own business too. Charlie and I have been talking about it. We got another guy in with us too. That's the American dream, ain't it?" Bobby O'Boy was wearing a wide grin. "Little Irish kid works his way up. High school drop out takes on General Motors and Ford? Ain't that the way it's supposed to be?" Then suddenly the smile was gone and a thoughtful, even bitter expression crossed his face. "Everybody in this country thinks a guy who drops out is a punk, or a delinquent, or maybe an addict, somebody dangerous, right? They don't stop to think maybe a lot of us need the scratch, 'cause we don't want our old ladies scrubbing floors just so they can buy a little food to stay alive.

"School's okay for most kids, but a lot of 'em think jobs are a whole helluva lot more important than taking a bunch of tests or being told we're dummys every day of our lives. If they wanted me to finish school they'd have done better making Charlie my teacher and Salvatore the principal. Those guys know what it's like coming from a background like mine. They know how to look out for a young guy, how to treat him fairly, how to help him figure out his life for himself. Those people at school were so busy making sure we weren't accidentally sitting in some class with the smart kids where we weren't supposed to be, they forgot that maybe *we* had a few little problems of our own, like getting a job somewhere so we aren't forced to go into the rackets or start shooting dope! They didn't listen to guys like us, so we listened to each other. I wouldn't give you a penny for all those teachers I had. Even the good ones, they never really helped me. They just made sure I stayed out of trouble. That's all. I'd lay down my life for Charlie McInally. That guy says, step in front of the next car, man, I step, and I ain't even twenty. He's a friend. He ain't someone who goes around saying people are dumb all the time. He helps 'em. Helps 'em the way some people in this country who ain't got anything really need to be helped.

"So maybe I'll go back to some night school one day, but I tell you, having my mother sitting home during the day, taking care of *herself* for the first time in her life, having a little fun, that's a helluva lot more important to me than waking up every morning with my hands all clean, without grease, you know, and looking up at the wall at some useless high school diploma. Working here teaches you how to do your own arithmetic. And my arithmetic, which ain't anything like what they used to try to teach us, says, every day of school I didn't attend because I dropped out, is another day my mother's going to stay home healthy and alive. So you figure it out, whether I did the best thing or not at the time!"

It was from Mrs. Clarissa Gibbs, a teacher, that I learned that Theresa Engler had been absent from school. Presumably, Theresa was down with a cold. No one really missed her for several days. That was in October.

In November I inquired about her again. Mrs. Gibbs reported that Theresa had returned to school but had been absent quite often for weeks thereafter.

"Still sick?" I asked Mrs. Gibbs.

"Must be," she answered.

"How's she doing in school?"

"Fair."

'That bad?"

"Worse."

"She afraid she may flunk?"

"She must be by now. Wouldn't have to be, if she'd just keep coming."

"Is it too late?"

"Not at all."

"Think I better talk to her?"

"It might be good."

"You ever talk to her about it?"

"There's no time, Tom. I've got twenty-six Theresa Englers. Some of them far worse too."

They've got so many in these schools, I thought, leaving the chilly junior high school that afternoon, that they can't keep track of who's here and who isn't. Strange that with attendance and order their paramount concerns, a child could be absent so frequently and her absence not be noticed.

The next day I visited the records office where the mother of a friend of mine guarded the vital statistics of the children. Mrs. Brenda Milan did me a favor and let me see Theresa's folder. Besides the attendance sheets was a letter from Theresa's mother requesting that the child be excused from school on two consecutive days because of the death of her grandfather and a slip of paper indicating she had had a fight in gym and was placed on a type of mild probation: no sports or library privileges for three days. Her aptitude scores varied from the twentieth to the eightieth percentile. Her verbal ability was fine, her mathematics aptitude nowhere near as high. Just like most of my friends.

"What are you mumbling over there? ' Brenda Milan asked.

"Nothing, other than making sure all my friends have the same learning hang-ups that I do. I get nervous when I see kids with high math scores."

"Engler have one?"

"No."

"Doesn't seem the type."

"That's one of the reasons I like her," I said. "She reminds me of me."

"Yeah. I'll bet she does." Brenda's sarcastic tone was obvious. She saw not one similarity in the world between Theresa Engler, a twelve-year-old black girl from one of Boston's poorest neighborhoods, and me.

Of the twenty or so school days in October Theresa Engler had missed fifteen. In the first week and a half of November she attended school once.

"You seen this kid around in the last weeks?" I asked Brenda.

"How would I know who I've seen? There are millions of Theresa Englers in the school."

I thanked her and left the cubby-sized office.

What, is there an echo in there? The teacher has twenty-six Theresa Englers, and the registrar's assistant has a million of them. The school would just as soon run with 25 percent absent, particularly if that 25 percent "makes trouble," which of course they do, otherwise why would they stay away from school in the first place? What a fantastic system, the public school. The second floor hasn't the faintest idea what the first floor is doing.

A little boy passed me, freezing cold in a windbreaker that could not be closed because the zipper had been torn off. "Hey kid, you know an Engler family that lives around here?"

"Uh, uh."

"This is Robinson Place, though, isn't it?"

"I don't know."

The cold and darkness depressed me. There were no addresses on most of the buildings, and it looked as if no one were inside any of them. The little boy was already at the corner, fifty yards ahead of me. There aren't a million Theresa Englers in the world. There are ten hundred billion of them. What if Theresa Engler were dead?

Eighty-eight Robinson Place—it was the right address. I remembered it now. Eight months ago when I was here, they were putting in sheets of plywood over the windows of the first-floor apartment, where there had been a fire. That afternoon a group of children wrote their names and all sorts of sayings on the wood. Then it was painted over, and three weeks later the children wrote and carved the same names and the same words in almost the same places. One of those children was Theresa Engler. She had written, "I love you, and I love me too. Theresa Engler." Her words were still visible.

I looked up the stairwell toward the third floor. "There's only one of you, Theresa Engler," I whispered. "Please believe that. Be up there."

I was standing at the door of the Engler's apartment. The light on the third floor was so dim I could barely see the other doors. A small sign had been pasted on the wall near the Engler's door, but the poor light prevented me from reading it. I could make out only the big letters at the top. "TO RESIDENTS OF THIS BUILDING."

I knocked softly. The door swung open, and Mrs. Titus Freemont, Theresa's grandmother, recently widowed, stood before me. She remembered my visits to this home months before and was pleased to see me, although she knew it was Theresa I had come to visit. She called for her granddaughter in the manner one might announce that a special delivery letter had just arrived. I hadn't moved from my spot in the doorway.

Theresa emerged from the kitchen. She wore jeans and a man's shirt and was barefoot. She said "Hi" without smiling and stopped about ten feet from where I stood, waiting for me to speak. It seemed as though she hadn't the slightest idea why I had come.

"How've you been?" I began.

"Okay."

"Everything okay and fine?" I smiled at Mrs. Freemont.

Theresa nodded.

"You aren't saying that because came, are you?"

"No."

"I thought maybe you were disappointed, like you were expecting somebody else." I tried to smile again. Theresa didn't say a word.

"Well, ask the man to step inside," Mrs. Freemont admonished her granddaughter. "Don't just make him stand there looking foolish." Theresa stepped into the living room and I entered the apartment.

"You came 'cause I ain't been in school?" she asked me at last. Her tone was utterly flat as if she couldn't care less about my response.

"Well, as a matter of fact I did ask Mrs. Gibbs about you."

"She say I wasn't coming, right?"

"Well, she did, yes. Have you?"

"She don't care if I come or not," Theresa said softly.

"I think maybe she does," I replied.

Mrs. Freemont was growing more interested in our conversation. She turned to face Theresa.

"She don't care for nobody 'cepting herself," Theresa said bitterly. "I was gone from there two weeks 'fore she knew somebody was missing. My friends told her. I was there when the other kids were out. Everybody knows. She don't care." Theresa looked about the room to avoid my eyes.

"Theresa, I feel badly about coming over and putting you on the spot . . ."

"What do you mean, on the spot?" she interrupted.

"I mean, you know, questioning you like some policeman with a suspect." I smiled kindly.

"You ain't no policeman," she said.

"No, I know I'm not, I merely wanted to ask if there was a problem with school. Is there something I can do? Would you like to talk about something?"

Minister, interviewer, truant officer, registrar, therapist, it all seems to come down to the same inane questions, the same brittle uneasiness and self-consciousness.

"You can talk to the man." Mrs. Freemont moved closer to Theresa.

"Ain't got nothing to tell him."

"I think maybe you do," Mrs. Freemont encouraged the girl gently. Her directness contrasted strongly with my own shying away from the problem. "Tell him what's been bothering you about the school."

"Ain't got nothing to tell him. Nothing bothering me neither."

"You're lying," Mrs. Freemont said sternly.

"I'd like to hear," I said.

"Nothing to hear. Got nothing to say. And I *ain't* lying."

"Hey, Theresa, you know what I think?" I began.

"No."

"I think that if I were in your shoes—'course you're not wearing shoes," I grinned, hoping to evoke a smile from her, but she didn't move a muscle. "Well, if I were you, and some guy came into *my* house and started asking me questions about why I hadn't been going to school, I wouldn't tell him a thing. I'd think, who the hell does he think he is coming over here poking around in my business. You know what I mean?"

She nodded her head. That was all. Not a word came from her, not a trace of a smile, not a hint of anything that would make me believe we could be friends. Theresa and I were stalemated, but Mrs. Freemont's anger was rising.

"You got this man come all the way over from your school—you ain't a truant officer are you?" she asked me.

"No, ma'm."

"There you are. He comes here trying to take an interest in you, and you just going to stand there and not say anything to him? You ain't never going to have a better chance than you got right now, little girl. If you want my opinion, you better start your talking and you better start right away before this man decides he's had enough with all your being quiet and decides to get himself out of here."

"Nothing to talk about," Theresa mumbled.

"You mean you're going to let the chance go by, just like that?" Mrs. Freemont persisted.

"I don't know what you're talking about," Theresa replied. One could see she felt betrayed. "You like him so much *you* talk to him. I ain't missing no chances with nobody. He ain't got no chances to give me even if I wanted some. You a friend of Mrs. Gibbs?"

"Not really," I answered. "I know her, of course."

"But you talked about me with her."

"I did. It started when I asked about where you were and Mrs. Gibbs said you'd been missing more and more days of school. That's the whole story. I asked if there was something wrong, and she didn't know. So I decided to come over here and make sure you were all right and see if I could help."

"What do you mean help?" In all this time Theresa hadn't moved. She stood facing me holding her hands in front of her.

"I don't know. If you want me I'm at your service."

"What's that mean?"

"He wants to help, Theresa," Mrs. Freemont was steaming mad, which made it easier for me to appear calm. Had she not been there I probably would have begun to reveal my own frustrations.

"Hey, Theresa," I said, "I got an idea. Okay?" She didn't budge. "Want to at least hear it."

"I ain't moving, am I?"

"Look. I think my coming here wasn't the greatest idea. I've seen you, so I know you're perfectly fine . . ."

"You thought I was sick?"

"I didn't know."

"I ain't sick."

"I can see that."

"You're going to get whipped talking like that," Mrs. Freemont warned her.

"You ain't going to touch me," Theresa challenged her grandmother.

"You belong in school," the older woman said, her eyes gleaming with hurt and outrage.

"I belong anywhere I want to belong. More my house than yours."

Mrs. Freemont looked at me wanting to apologize.

"It's all right," I said. "Let me finish. You said you'd at least hear my idea, Theresa."

"Go," she said sharply.

"You mean leave?" I pointed over my shoulder at the door.

Theresa smiled for the first time. It was a timorous smile, almost as though she was sorry for letting it happen, but she couldn't control herself. "I don't mean leave. You say 'go' when you want someone to go on talking. You say 'go.'"

I felt relieved and made a face at Mrs. Freemont to suggest my stupidity and age. She just shook her head. "My idea is this. Think about the school thing. If you'd like me to come back and talk we can do that. Or, we can go to Grumpy's for a hamburger. Maybe you'd even like some of the other kids to come along. Then again, if you don't want anything, you just have to keep quiet."

"I'll probably keep quiet," Theresa said barely loud enough for us to hear.

"But you got to promise me that if you want me you'll call." My words sounded like they had been uttered by a television actor. "Will you promise me?"

"We don't have a telephone so how'm I going to call you?"

I stared at her. This small matter, this mere figure of speech was what the whole afternoon had come to. The surveying of families, the door-by-door hunt to find out how many children live there, how many are of school age, how many in fact presently are in school leads to this, a child without a phone. The talks with teachers, the requests made to registrars, a peak at attendance records, the discovery that a single child, not a percentage, but merely this one girl has been out of school for weeks, the anger, the fright, the cold outside, the growing antipathy for almost anybody who doesn't see the world exactly as you see it, leads to the most mundane and yet most complex predicament: She has no phone; she can't call me. I looked at Mrs. Freemont, but she wouldn't allow her eyes to meet mine.

"I'll come back, Theresa," I said. "You think about whether I can help. A week from today I'll bang on the door. You answer it and either let me in or slam it in my face." Once again I hoped that I might be able to make her feel less anxious. "That a deal?"

"Okay."

"You open it wide or slam it shut."

"Slam it shut most likely."

"Well, we'll see."

"Yeah. Can I go now?" she looked back and forth between her grandmother and me.

"I don't have anything else, except to say that I'd like to see you go to school or clear up any problem that might be keeping you out."

"Ain't no problem keeping me out." Theresa turned and walked from the room. I heard her handling some pans in the kitchen, and then she moved on to the room beyond it and closed the door. My visit was merely a routine interruption on a cold afternoon. She had met her responsibility and disappeared.

"I'll be back in a week, Mrs. Freemont." I moved toward the door. I was wet with perspiration and dreading going back out in the cold.

"I heard what you told her." Mrs. Freemont was shaking her head as she reached to open the door for me. "She's in a bad way, my child is." She was totally unconcerned by the possibility that her words might reach Theresa in the rear of the apartment. "I know you did your best. We're all fretting over her staying out of school the way she is. Won't talk to nobody about it. Every once in a while, maybe, she'll let out some of her ideas, but most of the time she doesn't say a word. Makes it tougher that way, is what I tell her, but you see the way she is."

"She's feeling all right though, isn't she?"

"Like to think I felt as good as her. She's perfect. Young, never catches a cold. Wouldn't know what a pain was. Funny how some of these children like her growing up in places like this should be so healthy. Lots of the children don't even make it to her age. Die a whole lot younger from illness. Not her. She's never going to be sick."

"You think she's got some friends that, you know, she messes around with?" My question could not have been more ambiguous and yet at the same time offensive.

"No." Mrs. Freemont shook her head. She swept her hand through the air. "Theresa wouldn't do anything wrong. She wouldn't let no bully push her into doing something she didn't want to do. I know her too well for that. She's her own person, if you know what I mean. You tell her, clean the kitchen; she'll do it all right, but only when she's damn good and ready. Maybe now, maybe two days from now. I've learned to stay out of her hair. You force her into something you'll never see it get done. You saw that."

"I tried my best to go softly . . ."

"I thought you did all right. You weren't never going to win with her. You could tell that just by the way she was standing there looking at you. Big old steam engine could have knocked broadside into this building, brought down its front wall, and she wouldn't have moved any. I know that side of her. Better even than her mother knows. But she's feeling things. I can see that too, even if she doesn't move or say much. She's feeling everything."

"I know she is."

Mrs. Freemont looked thoughtful. Her eyes moved quickly as though she were reading a secret document.

"You know what's bothering her, don't you?" I asked.

"You mean why she doesn't go to her school? Yes, I think I do."

"Can you tell?" I looked over her shoulder toward the kitchen. There was no sound in the apartment.

"I'll tell," Mrs. Freemont sighed. "I don't know if it does any good, but I'll tell. She won't go because she's ashamed that we ain't got anything, in the way of material things I mean. She's afraid that folks will find out just how poor she is, and she don't want them knowing anything about that. Girl has only got a couple of dresses, and after she wore them day after day she thought she shouldn't go to school anymore. People would be laughing at her, she said, 'cause she always looked the same. Same goes for her shoes. She says they look funny and the other kids there, you know, going to laugh at them. She says they look like boy's shoes. I heard her say once, too, that the children go to the cafeteria at lunchtime, and she never has any money to buy things. She's always hungry and she doesn't have the nerve to ask them for money, otherwise like I told you, they'll see how bad off she is. Then another thing. She used to like to talk in class. It never seemed to bother her. Not like me. I still shiver thinking about what it must be like to have all those people looking at you while you're standing up there reciting something. But not Theresa. She'd go on and on, least that's what she said. But then this Mrs. Gibbs woman started to ask the children about their homes and their families, and what it's like outside of school."

"Theresa told you this?"

"This much she did, yes. 'Cause she came home one night crying about something, and when I finally got her quieted down—I had to put her in the bed she was so upset— she told me about what happened. See, the teacher didn't know what she was doing. I mean it wasn't *her* fault or anything." Mrs. Freemont was quick to make an apology. "But she must have started something going in that child's head. You could see it. She knew they'd get around to her, and she'd have to tell them about this house, and the street, and us too. She must have got scared, or ashamed, like I said before. She couldn't do it. I think that's when she stopped going."

"Like in October?"

"Just about then, yes," Mrs. Freemont agreed. "I don't know for certain, you understand, but I think that must have set her off. I know what she wants is to keep all of us away. She doesn't think they'd like her, if they knew we weren't doing so well."

"She's ashamed," I whispered.

"You can see how that might be."

"But what about the other kids?" I asked "They come from this area too. No one in the school is what anybody would call rich."

"Theresa knows that, but it don't make a difference. She was happy in her old school but something about this new place frightens her. I know she can't be herself there. She can't come from poor folks there. Something else she said. She goes to school now in a new building. You been there?"

"Yes I have. It's terribly handsome. Lots of bright rooms and colors . . ."

"Well see, I think that makes her nervous being in that fancy school. She doesn't feel it's the right place for her."

"You mean she likes the old place?" I accentuated my disbelief. "It's going to fall down any minute, Mrs. Freemont. It isn't even safe in there for the kids. It's a firetrap."

"Maybe. I ain't never seen it. But if I know that girl she'd tell you it was more in keeping with the sort of thing she's used to. She don't know what to do with all these new buildings and rugs like they got in that new school. She goes there and sees all that and comes home every day and sees all this," she gestured about the room with her hand. "Makes her head spin. She knows where she belongs. Fancy place ain't for her. I can understand that."

I didn't answer. I imagined Theresa standing alone before a huge closet with two dresses hanging in it and two pairs of shoes on the floor, deciding what to wear and then where she could run that day to pass the time while her friends went to the fancy school with the light oak shelving and burnt orange carpeting.

"Sometimes, you know," Mrs. Freemont reminded me, "folks don't like to move out of what they call their normal class. Some folks think if you dress up a girl like Theresa maybe she won't have those feelings anymore. But you could make her a queen, and she'd still be unhappy thinking people were going to find out all her secrets, like where she comes from and what her true home looks like. This here's our house, don't you see, and she's comfortable here. She can't just walk over to that new school thinking some teacher's going to make her write a story about how she grew up and all. If they want her to come back, they might have to come and get her." She looked sternly at me. "You see what I'm talking about to you? That child's afraid. She's afraid 'cause she feels ashamed. Nothing she did, nothing anybody did. But she feels it and no one's going to take that feeling away from her without one big battle."

"You're trying though, aren't you?" I asked respectfully.

Mrs. Freemont looked down. Her expression turned to sadness, although one could see determination in her face as well.

"We're talking about it almost every day. We have our meetings together in her room. She tells me a little, you know, and I tell her a little. I haven't got a whole lot to say about my own schooling. Wasn't much to it, I'm afraid."

"I'd like to help too, if I can."

"I know that. I could see that in the way you were talking to Theresa before."

"I didn't do too well though, did I?"

"She can be stubborn when she wants to."

"And you can be very diplomatic, Mrs. Freemont."

She looked away modestly. "We're all working on this. But there's no sense forcing her. You don't have the feelings she carries in her heart just because someone says something, calls you a bad name, you know. You got those feelings because something's gone wrong your whole life. Every minute you looked out over the world you see it was wrong. That's what she's got in her heart. Fills up her whole body too. That girl in there is a child out of school because she's taken a long look at the world and decided the world don't want her. Don't want even the smallest part of her. Not even the school part. Other kids, maybe they feel it, maybe they don't, but she's special. She's a very special little girl. It ain't intelligence and it ain't something anyone has the right to blame her for. Shame is more like what it is. All over her body that child feels a shame. That's why her clothes are so important to her, and how she looks and talks and sounds to other folks is so important. Folks at school don't have the time just to listen to her and think about what might be causing her all her troubles. They got way too many children there for them to just be worrying about this one or that one. You're a busy man too. All of us are busy. We all got our jobs, no matter where we are. Hell, we got jobs even when we don't have jobs." Mrs. Freemont laughed aloud. She wanted to make it easier for me.

"Should I come back?"

"You could try. I ain't promising anything."

"But you aren't going to force her to go to school, if she doesn't want to, are you?" It was a rhetorical question.

"I ain't about to force nobody to do anything against their wishes, 'specially no child who knows what that child in there knows. And feels too."

"Will you call me if I can help?"

Mrs. Freemont stood facing me, a gentle smile on her face. She looked quickly to where Theresa had stood when Theresa announced that the Englers had no phone.

"I'll come back," I promised.

"Anytime." The word was said with finality.

I opened the door and began buttoning my coat. My arms and back were coated with perspiraton. I wanted just one more exchange, a pleasant good-bye, a hopeful remark perhaps. "Say, Mrs. Freemont, I noticed the little sign on the other side of the door out here in the hall. I didn't mean to pry, but I wondered whether it was something important." I went around the corner and squinted in the darkness at the words, "TO RESIDENTS OF THIS BUILDING." "Is it anything important?"

She stood in the doorway and pulled lightly at the wide belt she was wearing. "Says that the building's going to be torn down one of these days real soon."

"When?"

"Don't say. Just says it's going to be real soon."

I looked back in the darkness at the sign. "Does it say anything about their finding new places for the tenants to live in?"

"No sir," she answered, the muscles of her face perfectly still. "Don't say nothing about that."

"This happen before to, you know, to the family? You and the Englers? Theresa?"

"This time's going to be number four. Guess you could say we ain't the luckiest family going, are we?"

We faced each other a long time before she closed the door.

5.

The Work of
Reinstatement

By now everyone knows that educational institutions, like the practice of psychotherapy, have the potential of dealing with issues no less significant than life and death. When human beings are involved, life and death are involved. And when these people are children born in poverty, then, irrespective of what television shows and magazines might like us to believe about happy, close-knit poor families, the heart of the matter is the life and death of these children. Sadly, too many schools have followed the pattern of governments and grand administrators. They would have done better following the secret traditions of medicine, although not the bureaucracies of hospitals.

The phrase "death of the spirit" has been so diluted in contemporary rhetoric that few of us take literally the truthfulness of it. Just as some people continue to doubt the realities of living and dying that underlie psychology and psychiatry, others continue to doubt the therapeutic and health-giving capabilities of schools. The problem is that we cannot judge a school in a poor county merely by glancing at it quickly. There is no tourism when the feelings and strains of poverty are at stake. A peek inside a decaying school, a short visit with a hurt child is only the beginning, the outermost layer. It is, as many have said, the hour-by-hour poverty without recourse, without the slightest chance of looking beyond it that kills the spirit of children and their parents. It is probably a wise merchandising formula to marry words like death and school, but in truth death *can* be bred in schools.

Again, the question is, do schools in the end really matter? The answer is they most assuredly do. They matter in the beginning too, because they have power, the power to give life and take it away. They draw this power from society, from the rich and the mighty, from the poor and the weak; and they use it. The culture allows it; the people condone it; history hardly bats an eye. When school is good the child may flourish; when it is bad, the child is severely weakened. Each day matters to a school. Each day matters to the child as well, for a change of plan or of heart is more difficult to undertake when one feels broken by shame and separated from the world's wealth, a wealth that ought to have some of its roots in school.

We have inherited a fragmented culture, a collection of human groupings where the chance for life in one is not matched in another, and the potential for full development, maximum vigor, and ripeness found in one is not possible in another. The very words we use, often, to derogate the young, like selfish and self-centered, are precisely how we should be described, as we wittingly or unwittingly work to preserve this fissured array of peoples, this precarious system of human relationships.

If there is a seeming immaturity in the cognitive, social, or psychological skills of the children heard in this book, if there is a presumed "slow down" in their growth rates, if the socialization that we expect to happen because of their experiences in schools does not take place, then we had better look not only to the children and their families, but beyond to their communities, and then beyond to our communities and to our economic and political systems, which ultimately are the source of these young people's inability to move on to mature levels. Ironically, we have to do this extra looking, because in their cocoon of solipsism, a cocoon an entire culture helps to weave, some of these young people are able to see only their own development. They imagine that they alone are responsible for their evolution, that their slowness and inability to achieve devolves only on themselves. This cannot be true. We too must take responsibility for their evolution, their development.

What, then, do we recommend to alleviate the problem of children excluded from school.

There are, as always, two sources of change, two bodies of power: the government, acting at the federal, state, and community level, and the people, the millions of parents whose children attend school or have been excluded from school. As the Children's Defense Fund report states, the federal government must establish committees to oversee exclusion cases and, more importantly, devise ways for children to be reinstated. The government, most likely through its Department of Health, Education, and Welfare, must not only keep exact records of exclusion, it must demand that school systems honor all nondiscrimination laws. In this sense, the government must monitor school districts' policies on exclusion. Similarly, every branch of the government connected with civil rights legislation must monitor school districts in order to be certain that discrimination against racial and ethnic minority children, as well as national origin minority children, is not practiced. The treatment of pregnant girls by many school districts, as we saw in Chapter 2, suggests that discrimination against female students also is practiced in schools and also must be prohibited. This too is a task for government.

When one speaks of such monitoring programs, one is speaking not only of collecting information but using it to end exclusion, notably through government funding, which remains the major source of money to schools. Importantly, in guarding against illegal exclusion and discrimination, the government must watch carefully that it protects students' rights to privacy and maintains confidentiality of their records.

To ask federal and local governments to demand accountability from the projects they fund is hardly a new suggestion. But until this is done assiduously, millions of children will remain out of school, and billions of dollars will be misspent, openly squandered. We have already noted instances where money earmarked for special education or bilingual programs ends up refurbishing school programs in which too few or no poor, minority, or non-English-speaking students benefit. The responsibility for seeing that all children are granted their right to public education lies with the people of this country as well as within the government. Every parent, as the age-old chant goes, must be involved. Being informed of the laws and policies of school districts and then making certain that these laws are enacted to protect children is, in fact, part of the social revolution every educational reformer demands.

In the case of children excluded from school, one repeatedly finds parents admitting ignorance of the law. No one has advised them of their rights; no one has told them what to do. Furthermore, as we have seen, many of the conditions that lead to nonenrollment—for example, deficiency in English, pregnancy, or mental retardation—are precisely what some parents want to deny or hide. Understandably, they feel better keeping children with these problems out of school. No one knows, then, of the condition. Census-takers and survey researchers are led to overlook them; more significantly, school systems are allowed to continue their exclusionary and discriminatory practices. The irony of this silence and nonaction is that excluded children tend to live in communities characterized by their poverty or high number of minority students. If a few parents began to push for their children's rights, for the special needs of their children, other parents surely would be encouraged to join them. Indeed, this movement has already started. Many long ago began this push for inclusion in school, often making profound changes in school systems, more often being repulsed and denied assistance by legal and educational groups.

Anyone who has worked to get children back in school is familiar with the forms of bureaucratic resistance: "Parents shouldn't make a fuss. They don't know the facts. What are parents even talking about? There's not exclusion of children from schools going on. Your child is the exception; the problem is not severe. The parents may have a point, but other problems take precedence, and besides, the exclusion issue isn't in our jurisdiction. The parents' demand is reasonable, it just comes too soon; the children will have to wait. The problem requires further study and more money. And, finally, if we help *your* kid, we'd have to help them all."

Embedded in these statements are the issues parents must attack. Who are the children out of school from one's community? From one's child's classroom? Why are they out? What is a school's budget, and how is the money being spent? What is the fate of every child out of school? Who is attending to them? Everyone in the multibillion-dollar education business must be held accountable. Children are not merely falling through policy or budgetary cracks; they are being discriminated against, neglected, abused, kept out of school. But to work on the problem of excluded children means commitment—that inevitable word. It means working with schools until every child is enrolled. It means collaborating with school officials, principals, teachers, attendance officers, record-keepers. It means calling in higher officials. It means leaning on people.

Of those children excluded from school, about 11 percent of the cases can be traced directly to suspension. There are far too many suspensions, and far too many for acts that do not warrant them. The statistics of suspended children confirm the inequitable treatment of poor and minority children, while the individual life studies we have examined reveal the often arbitrary nature of the suspension process and the violation of the student's fundamental rights.

Beyond the statistics and the life studies lies the question of what happens to children suspended from school. We know that even short-term punishment of this kind may lead to permanent exclusion. We know as well that there are too few programs aimed at helping children out of school for three, eight, fifteen days at a time. In some cases, surely, suspensions lead to a renewed communication between a student and his or her school and teach the student a significant lesson about authority, discipline, and social order. In most cases, however, suspensions are worthless and ultimately hurtful. In this regard, suspension for the act of truancy is not only foolish in its redundancy, it is a ludicrous settlement.

Like corporal punishment, arbitrary suspension policies and suspensions without hearings or negotiations are widespread in this country. Children's rights are denied in these suspension procedures, and ameliorative alternatives are ignored, although recent Supreme Court decisions should improve this condition. Just as there are well-codified regulations to protect schools and their personnel, so must there be clearly stated and well-conceived guidelines for student discipline. Importantly, the well-being of people—not just powerful people, older people, or bigger people—must be given the highest priority. At present the hundreds of thousands of unjust and often illegal suspension cases testify to the fact that we continue to indulge in our primitive impulse to get rid of people who deviate from our patterns of authority and order. We strip them of their rights and privileges no matter what the cost to them, and ultimately to us.

The Children's Defense Fund's recommendations in the area of school suspension are to be seconded:

1. Every school board and administration must reexamine existing disciplinary and suspension policies. This includes a reconsideration of policy when violence to property has been committed. Criminal acts must be punished, but it must be remembered that violent behavior is at the root of only a small minority of suspension cases.

2. Emergency grounds for exclusion should be clearly stated and disseminated.

3. All suspensions must require a hearing, where all parties involved may state their case. The idea is old, the practice rarely followed, and in some schools never at all. Everything we know about suspension, furthermore, should convince us that it is a useless and ultimately destructive punitive device. It is the very last resort.

4. Parents must watch closely that all varieties of teaching styles and procedures are instituted in schools and that none of these styles is in any way discriminatory. This means parents

becoming implicated in the selection of policy-makers, principals, and superintendents. It also means learning how records are kept and statistics compiled. When it comes to discriminating and exclusionary action, the mathematics is simple: If even one child is excluded from school, something is wrong.

In the light of discriminatory action, we reprint a passage from the Emergency School Aid Act:

> No educational agency should be eligible for assistance in the Civil Rights Act of 1974 (Title VI) if . . . it has had or maintains in effect any practice, policy or procedure which results or have resulted in . . . imposing disciplinary sanctions, including expulsions, suspensions, or corporal or other punishment, in a manner which discriminates against minority group children on the basis of race, color, or national origin.

In response to those who, in desperation shake their head and mutter, "There ought to be a law," one may often reply, there *is* a law, and in many instances it is written in a style nonlawyers can understand. Instituting the law is something else; it's a full-time job of the people.

In the case of handicapped children, the recommendations are not dissimilar. To begin, the children must be found and reinstated in school, if not enrolled for the first time. In Oregon and Illinois outreach programs were instituted as part of legislative bills. In both states door-to-door surveys resulted in the locating of hundreds of handicapped children. Programs of this sort are easily launched and require the collaboration of parents and professionals.

The next step is to reevaluate all classification and diagnostic procedures used with handicapped children. This means reevaluating not only all existing tests but the use to which these tests are put. In the short and long run, test results yield labels that affect not only the child's placement in or out of school, but the child's self-image as well. Children feel elated when they receive high grades and promising achievement scores; the problem is that too many children receive statistically based labels like moron, retarded, learning disabled, or uneducable. From the instant of labeling, their entire educational histories are altered, usually for the worse. Given the inadequate nature of most tests, one might do well to consider abolishing them entirely. If Wechsler himself is uncertain of the meaning of intelligence, then we had better lay aside these exploratory instruments. If they are maintained, however, then it is imperative that we work with the children who are diagnosed as needing special help and not neglect or openly discriminate against them. Presumably, physicians discovering high blood pressure, hearing loss, or cardiac imperfections do something to improve the health of their patients.

Again the Children's Defense Fund recommendations for planning school assessments of students should be repeated here and widely instituted:

1. Many kinds of people should be used in assessing children.
2. Many kinds of procedures should be used in assessing children.
3. The focus must be on the child's behavior in a variety of settings.
4. There must be continuous evaluation of the child.

The important point is that all the evaluations and labeling in the world do no good if the child's needs are not met. We know very little about someone who scores 107 on an IQ test, other than that IQ score. And what does that mean. As Judah Schwartz reminds us, tests only *indicate* that certain behavior of an intellectual or psychological nature was evoked. They never *demonstrate* that that certain behavior *cannot* be evoked. Everyone is educable. Everyone has God-given valuable capacities, as well as the potential to have these capacities enhanced. Trite lines, probably, for those who read books on education, but abiding beliefs among people excluded from school.

As a final point on classification and diagnosis, it is fitting and necessary that whenever possible, parents and their children partake in all assessment procedures. Every aspect of the process must be made clear to all parties, every proposed procedure outlined exactly. Parents must know what special needs their children have and how these needs will be met by the school. Parents, moreover, must have complete access to their child's records and be guaranteed rights of privacy and confidentiality. They must also retain the right to refuse the procedures recommended for their child. (One is tempted to suggest that hospitals should follow this same program when dealing with patients or the parents of patients. One can just hear the response to such a suggestion, "Can you imagine schools and hospitals having to run this way?" But can anyone defend the way schools and hospitals presently are allowed to run?)

A note of recommendation to schools excluding pregnant girls: Pregnancy in no way turns young women into nonhumans. An eternally natural process, pregnancy must not ever be grounds for open dismissal or even subtle degradation. Supportive services like counseling and information on pre- and postnatal care might well be offered to young women, but all of this information should be available to all students. A young woman's pregnancy is only disruptive in a classroom if the sociology of that classroom allows for disruption. Pegnancy also can be the basis of inquiries into biology, sex education, anthropology, child development, genetics, literature. If the pregnant girl is viewed as a freak—as retarded, physically handicapped, non-English-speaking children, and nocturnal bed-wetters invariably are—then undoubtedly her presence in class will be disruptive. If she is viewed as a person experiencing special physical and emotional changes, then daily educational programs can not only proceed, they can be enriched.

In all these recommendations, one asks for compassion, commitment, hard work. Of course the government must help with substantial programs and substantial fundings. No doubt, too, well-heeled political and economic systems create and perpetuate the problem of children out of school. The poor and minorities have always been shortchanged and rendered powerless. There is no profit to be earned, someone once remarked, from investing in poverty. But while others more competent than I outline and institute the plans for the largest-scale changes of all, some of us are left to work with the children in and out of school.

Despite their bureaucratic character, schools have always been places where change may occur. There are always administrators, teachers, volunteers, students, parents with whom one can collaborate on the problem of exclusion. All of the children whose voices are heard in this book were reinstated in school. In truth, the reinstatement proceedings were not all that difficult. Many school officials actually were surprised that anyone came forward to help the children, and without the threat of law suits, the children were allowed to return. Their progress now is watched rather carefully. There has been no further trouble.

To say that our public schools need restructuring is an understatement. But to say that, given their shabby state, it may be better for children to be out of school is nonsense, the idle speculation of people who have never met excluded children, never heard their stories.

Indeed, one of the most serious problems we face is that so many policymakers and psychological testers, theoreticians and critics of all types never have to look into the eyes of the people whose lives they are trying to shape and control. They never have to hear these children and their parents talk; they never have to encounter the myriad forms of competence and talent that these millions of people reveal. Too many of us know of families of excluded children by the very labels and test scores we ourselves generate for them. To think of them in this manner is more than a denial of the humaness of human beings; it is a form of oppression.

In the end the temptation of many of us in the position of writer, critic, consultant, is to find some new answer or product, some new approach or innovative program. Even in a nonaction-oriented sense we crave new metaphors, new perspectives. Another report on children out of school is called just that—another report. We've heard it before, goes the reaction. It's important, maybe the most important problem facing us in education, but it's not new.

Given the advertising and production nature of contemporary society, given our present technologies, I understand the response. I recognize that prestigious scientists, like prestigious industries and universities, are the first to perform experiments and initiate programs. Less prestigious people usually are left to replicate these experiments and programs, if not simply copy them. The remainder of society lives with whatever lasts and with whatever is overlooked. Some architects adore renovation; the majority prefer to be given an expanse of ground and be told, "Create!"

This point is extremely relevant in considering the exclusion of children from school. Surely, whole new ideas and procedures are needed to reroute the evolution of our school system and the development of our children. Nevertheless, it is the same old set of problems, issues, circumstances that stay with us. More grievous, it is the same families, the same human groups facing the same realities.

The political dangers of intelligence testing, the system of tracking students, refusing a foreign-born boy admission to school because his English is poor or a girl because she is pregnant, the lack of facilities for physically and emotionally ill children, suspensions for academic failures and behavioral misdemeanors, the day-by-day sense of shame and hurt engendered by poverty and racism, physiological stresses and the daily affronts to one's self-image are hardly "new" realities. Indeed, many would call them "old hat." But there are some people whose very lives seem to the rest of us to be old hat, precisely because there is nothing new about their circumstances or their anguish. It is the same anguish of their parents and grandparents, perhaps our grandparents as well. Their hurts have never receded; the dangers and pressures of their existence are historical replicas of those of their ancestors. So, while the exciting part of research, policy formation, architectural design, writing, may be the creative part of starting from scratch, the building free on endless allotments of space, the task for those of us who do not participate in the culture in this manner is to make certain that the conditions of oppression are not sustained and recreated in new forms for tomorrow's children.

Bibliography

The following list of books, articles, and reports is meant as an aid to the reader who seeks more information on the general topic of children excluded from school. There is, as one can readily see from even this highly incomplete list, a great deal of literature on the subject. Moreover, in order to familiarize oneself with the topic means reading in several areas of studies. These areas include child development, the social psychology of schooling, community organization and organizing, children's rights, poverty, the family, and the law. Some of the more well-known books and articles on these subjects appear in the following bibliography. In addition, the reader will find material on more specialized topics covered in this book. These include intelligence testing and psychological achievement testing generally, mental retardation, language development, juvenile delinquency, and mental health. It is difficult to say which of these references are the most important, indeed truly indispensable. All of the works were found to be valuable in the writing of this volume. Still, it might be said that in undertaking the sort of work described here, one must begin with a knowledge of the actual facts regarding the denial of children's rights and the laws covering these rights.

Alinsky, Saul. *Reveille for Radicals.* Chicago: University of Chicago Press, 1946. Second printing, New York: Vintage (1969).

_____ . *Rules for Radicals.* New York: Vintage (1972).

Allen, Vernon L. *Psychological Factors in Poverty.* Chicago: Markham, 1970.

Ames, Louise Bates. *Is Your Child in the Wrong Grade?* New York: Harper & Row, 1966.

_____ . *Stop School Failure.* New York: Harper & Row, 1972.

Anderson, Elizabeth. *The Disabled Schoolchild, A Study of Integration in Primary Schools.* London: Methuen, 1973.

Aries, Phillipe. *Centuries of Childhood.* New York: Vintage, 1962.

Ashton-Warner, Sylvia. *Teacher.* New York: Simon and Schuster, 1963.

Basic Rights of the Mentally Handicapped. Washington, D.C.: Mental Health Law Project, 1973.

Bay C. *The Structure of Freedom.* New York: Atheneum, 1965.

Becker, Howard S. *Outsiders: Studies in the Sociology of Deviance.* New York: Free Press, 1965.

Bernstein, Basil. "Social Class and Linguistic Development," in *Education, Economy & Society,* ed. A.H. Halsey, Floud, and Anderson. New York: Free Press, 1962.

Bietz, Charles, and Michael Washburn. *Creating the Future, A Guide to Living and Working for Social Change.* New York: Bantam, 1974.

Biklen, Douglas. *Let Our Children Go.* Syracuse, N.Y.: Human Policy Press, 1974.

Billingsley, Andrew. *Black Families in White America.* Englewood Cliffs, N.J.: Prentice Hall, 1968.

Birch, Herbert, and Joan Gussow. *Disadvantaged Children: Health, Nutrition and School Failure.* New York: Harcourt, Brace & World, 1970.

Birch, J., and G.D. Stevens. *Reaching the Mentally Retarded.* Indianapolis, Bobbs-Merrill, 1955.

Blatt, Burton. *Exodus From Pandemonium, Human Abuse and a Reformation of Public Policy.* Boston: Allyn and Bacon, 1970.

_____ and Fred Kaplan. *Christmas in Purgatory.* Boston : Allyn and Bacon, 1966.

_____ (editor). *Souls in Extremis.* Boston: Allyn and Bacon, 1973.

Blishen, Edward (editor). *The School That I'd Like.* London: Penguin, 1970.

Blodgett, Harriet. *Mentally Retarded Children: What Parents and Others Should Know.* Minneapolis: University of Minnesota Press, 1971.

Bragen, George, and Harry Specht. *Community Organizing.* New York: Columbia University Press, 1973.

Braginsky, D.D., and B.M. Braginsky. *Hansels and Gretels: Studies of Children in Institutions.* New York: Holt, Rinehart and Winston, 1971.

Bremner, Robert H. *From the Depths: The Discovery of Poverty in the United States.* New York: New York University Press, 1967.

_____ (editor). *Children and Youth in America—A Documentary History.* Cambridge, Mass.: Harvard University Press, 1971.

Butler, Robert A. "The Public High School Student's Constitutional Right to a Hearing," *Clearinghouse Review* 5 (1971): 454-464.

Chase, Naomi Feigelson. *A Child Is Being Beaten.* New York: Holt, Rinehart and Winston, 1975.

The Children Are Waiting. Report of the Early Childhood Development Task Force. New York: July 20, 1970.

Children's Defense Fund. *Children Out of School in America.* Report published by the Children's Defense Fund of the Washington Research Project, 1974.

"Children's Rights," *Saturday Review* (Oct. 23, 1971): 27.

"Children's Rights," *Trial Magazine* (May-June 1974).

Cohen, David, *et. al.* "Consumer Protection in Public Education." Cambridge, Mass: Center for the Study of Public Policy, 1971.

Cole, L. *Our Children's Keepers.* New York: Grossman, 1972.

Cole, Michael. *The Cultural Context of Learning and Thinking.* New York: Basic Books, 1971.

Coles, Robert. *Children of Crisis.* Boston: Atlantic-Little, Brown, 1967.

_____ . *Still Hungry in America.* New York: World, 1969.

_____ . *Migrants, Sharecroppers, Mountaineers. Children of Crisis,* vol. 2. Boston: Atlantic-Little, Brown, 1971.

_____ . *The South Goes North. Children of Crisis,* vol. 3. Boston: Atlantic-Little, Brown, 1971.

_____ and Maria Piers. *The Wages of Neglect.* New York: Quadrangle, 1969.

Cottle, Thomas J. "Matilda Rutherford: She's What You Would Call a Whore," *Antioch Review* 31 (Winter 1971-1972): 519-543.

_____ . *The Abandoners: Portraits of Loss, Separation and Neglect.* Boston: Little, Brown, 1972.

_____ . *Time's Children: Impressions of Youth.* Boston: Little, Brown, 1971.

_____. *The Voices of School: Educational Issues Through Personal Accounts.* Boston: Little, Brown, 1973.

———. *A Family Album: Portraits of Intimacy and Kinship.* New York: Harper & Row, 1974.

———. *Black Children, White Dreams.* Boston: Houghton Mifflin, 1974.

Cox, Fred M. *et al.* (editors). *Strategies of Community Organization.* Itasia, Ill.: Peacock, 1970.

Cronbach, Lee. *Essentials of Psychological Testing.* New York: Harper, 1949.

Dabrow, Allan M. and Daniel M. Migliore. "Juvenile Rights Under the Fourth Amendment," *Journal of Family Law* 11 (1972): 753-764.

"Declaration of the Rights of the Child," League of Nations, United Nations, 1924, 1948, 1959, *International Child Welfare Review* 22 (1968): 4-8.

Dennison, George. *The Lives of Children.* New York: Random House, 1970.

Des Jardins, Charlotte. *How to Move Bureaucracies.* Chicago: Coordinating Council for Handicapped Children, 1971.

Deutsch, Martin. "The Role of Social Class in Language Development and Cognition," *American Journal of Orthopsychiatry* 35 (January 1965): 78-88.

———. *The Disadvantaged Child.* New York: Basic Books, 1967.

——— and Bert Brown. "Social Influences in Negro-White Intelligence Differences," *Journal of Social Issues* 20 (1964): 24-35.

Dimond, Paul. "Towards a Children's Defense Fund," *Harvard Educational Review* 41 (August 1971): 3.

Directory of Resources on Early Childhood Education. ERIC, 1971. Reprint of Day Care and Child Development Council of America, 1971.

Divoky, Diane (editor). *How Old Will You be in 1984? Expressions of Outrage from the High School Free Press.* New York: Avon, 1971.

Dorman, Michael. *Under 21: A Young Peoples Guide to Legal Rights.* New York: Dell, 1970.

Douglas, J.W.B. *The Home and the School.* New York: Humanities Press, 1966.

Early Childhood Facilities/1: An Annotated Bibliography on Early Childhood. Architectural Research Laboratory of the University of Michigan, 1970. Available from Educational Facilities Laboratories, Inc.

Eliot, Martha M. "Six Decades of Action for Children," *Children Today* 1 (March-April 1972): 2.

Elmer, E. *Children in Jeopardy.* Pittsburgh: University of Pittsburgh Press, 1967.

Erikson, Erik. *Identity: Youth and Crisis.* New York: Norton, 1968.

Farber, B. *Mental Retardation: Its Social Context and Social Consequences.* Boston: Houghton Mifflin, 1968.

Farber, Jerry. *The Student as Nigger.* New York: Pocket Books, 1970.

Forer, Lois G. "The Rights of Children: The Legal Vacuum," *American Bar Association Journal* 55 (1969).

_____. "The Rights of Children," *Young Children* 27 (August 1972): 6.

Fontana, Vincent J. *The Maltreated Child Syndrome in Children.* Springfield, Ill.: Thomas, 1964.

Frazier, Nancy, and Myra Sadker. *Sexism in School and Society.* New York: Harper and Row, 1973.

Freire, Paul. *Pedagogy of the Oppressed.* New York: Herder and Herder, 1970.

Freud, Anna. *Normality and Pathology in Childhood: Assessments of Development.* New York: International Universities Press, 1966.

Frey, Martin A. "The Rights of Counsel in Student Disciplinary Hearings," *Valparaiso University Law Review* 5 (1970): 48-70.

Friedenberg, Edgar Z. *Coming of Age in America.* New York: Vintage, 1963.

Gardner, D.E.M. *The Education of Young Children.* New York: Barnes and Noble, 1956.

Gerzon, Mark. *A Childhood for Every Child.* New York: Outerbridge and Lagard, 1973.

Gil, David G. *Violence Against Children.* Cambridge, Mass.: Harvard University Press, 1970.

Glasser, William. *Schools Without Failure.* New York: Harper & Row, 1969.

Glazer, Nona Y., and Carol F. Creedon (editors). *Children and Poverty: Some Sociological and Psychological Perspectives.* Chicago: Rand-McNally, 1970.

Goffman, Erving. *Stigma: Notes on the Management of Spoiled Identity.* New York: Prentice-Hall, 1963.

Goodell, Carol (editor). *The Changing Classroom.* New York: Ballantine, 1973.

Goodman, Mary Ellen. *The Culture of Childhood.* New York: Teachers College Press, 1970.

Goodman, Paul (editor). *Children's Rights: Toward the Liberation of the Child.* New York: Praeger, 1971.

Gould, Richard M., Jr. "Children's Rights: More Liberal Games," *Social Policy* 1 (July-August 1971): 7.

Gottlieb, David (editor). *Children's Liberation.* Englewood Cliffs, N.J.: Prentice-Hall, 1973.

Graubard, Allen. *Free the Children: Radical Reform and Free School Movement.* New York: Vintage, 1973.

Great Atlantic and Pacific School Conspiracy. *Doing Your Own School: A Practical Guide to Starting and Operating a Community School.* Boston: Beacon Press, 1972.

Greene, Mary Frances, and Orlette Ryan. *The School Children: Growing up in Slums.* New York: Random House, 1966.

Gross, Beatrice, and Ronald Gross. *Radical School Reform.* New York: Simon and Schuster, 1970.

Grosser, Charles F. *New Directions in Community Organization: From Enabling to Advocacy.* New York: Praeger Publishers, 1973.

Guidelines for Collection, Maintenance and Dissemination of Pupil Records. Russell Sage Foundation, 230 Park Ave., New York, N.Y., 10017.

Guthrie, James, and Edward Wynne. *New Models for American Education.* New York: Prentice-Hall, 1971.

Hansen, Soren, and Jesper Jensen. *The Little Red Schoolbook.* New York: Pocket Books, 1971.

Harrison Grizzuti, Barbara. *Unlearning the Lie, Sexism in Schools.* New York: Morrow, 1974.

Harvard University Center for Law and Education. "Students Rights Litigation Packet." Cambridge, Mass., 1972.

Heisler, Verda. *A Handicapped Child in the Family: A Guide for Parents.* New York: Grune and Stratton, 1972.

Henry, Jules, *Culture Against Man.* New York: Random House, 1963.

Hentoff, Nat. *Our Children Are Dying.* New York: Viking, 1967.

Herndon, James. *The Way It Spozed to Be.* New York: Simon and Schuster, 1968.

———. *How to Survive in Your Native Land.* New York: Bantam, 1972.

Hess, Robert D. "The Transmission of Cognitive Strategies in Poor Families: The Socialization of Apathy and Underachievement." In *Psychological Factors in Poverty,* ed. Vernon L. Allen. Chicago: Markham, 1970.

Hill, B., and N. Burke. "Some Disadvantaged Youths Look at Their Schools," *Journal of Negro Education* 37 (1968): 135-139.

Hoffman, Banesh. *The Tyranny of Testing.* New York: Macmillan, 1964.

Hoffman, Herbert J. *Take A Giant Step.* Boston: Massachusetts Advisory Council on Education, 1970.

Holt, John. *Freedom and Beyond.* New York: Dell, 1973.

_____. *How Children Fail.* New York: Dell, 1972.

Huenefield, John. *The Community Activist's Handbook: A Guide to Organizing, Financing and Publicizing Community Campaigns.* Boston: Beacon Press, 1970.

Hunt, J. McV. *Intelligence and Experience.* New York: Ronald Press, 1961.

James, Howard. *Children in Trouble: A National Scandal.* New York: Pocket Books, 1971.

Jones, Ron W. *Finding Community: A Guide to Community Research and Action.* Palo Alto, Calif.: James E. Freel and Associates, 1971.

Jordon, June, and Terri Bush. *The Voice of the Children.* New York: Holt, Rinehart and Winston, 1970.

Kagan, Jerome. *Understanding Children: Behavior, Motives and Thought.* New York: Harcourt Brace Jovanovich, 1971.

Kahn, Alfred. *Social Policy and Social Services.* New York: Random House, 1973.

_____, Sheila Karmerman, and Brenda McGowan. *Child Advocacy Report of a National Baseline Study.* Washington, D.C.: U.S. Department of Health, Education, and Welfare, 1973.

Kahn, Si. *How People Get Power: Organizing Oppressed Communities For Action.* New York: McGraw Hill, 1970.

Katz, Michael. *Class, Bureaucracy and Schools: The Illusion of Educational Change in America.* New York: Praeger, 1971.

Katz, Sanford N. *When Parents Fail: The Law's Response to Family Breakdown.* Boston: Beacon Press, 1971.

Kemble, Bruce. *Give Your Child a Chance.* New York: Allen, 1970.

Kirk, Samuel A. *Educating Exceptional Children.* Boston: Houghton Mifflin, 1972.

Klapmuts, Nora. *Children's Rights.* Hackensack, N.J.: National Council on Crime and Delinquency, 1973.

Kohl, Herbert. *The Open Classroom.* New York: Random House, 1970.

———. *Reading, How To.* New York: Dutton, 1973.

———. *36 Children.* New York: New American Library, 1973.

Kohler, Mary. "The Rights of Children, An Unexplored Constituency," *Social Policy* 1 (March-April 1971): 6.

Kozol, Jonathan. *Death at an Early Age.* New York: Bantam Books, 1968.

Lawrence, Margaret M. Young.*Inner City Families.* New York: Human Science Press, 1975.

Lawton, D. *Social Class, Language and Education.* New York: Schocken, 1968.

"The Legal Rights of Secondary School Children Charged with an Act of Delinquency or Violation of School Rules." St. Louis, Mo.: St. Louis University School of Law, 1971.

Lemert, Edward M. *Social Action and Legal Change: Revolution Within the Juvenile Court.* Chicago: Aldine, 1970.

LeShan, Edna J. *The Conspiracy Against Childhood.* New York: Atheneum, 1967.

Levine, Murray, and Adeline Levine. *A Social History of Helping Services.* New York: Meredith, 1970.

Lippman, Leopold, and I. Ignacy Goldberg. *Right to Education: Anatomy of the Pennsylvania Case and Its Implications for Exceptional Children.* New York: Teachers College Press, 1973.

Lobenthal, Joseph S. *Growing Up Clean in America: A Guide to the Complexities of Being a Young American.* New York: World, 1970.

Lundberg, E.O. *Unto the Least of These: Social Services for Children.* New York: D. Appleton-Century Co., 1947.

Lurie, Ellen. *How to Change the Schools: A Parents Action Handbook on How to Fight the System.* New York: Vintage, 1970.

Manser, Ellen P. (editor). *Family Advocacy: A Manual for Action.* New York: Family Service Association of America, 1973.

Matza, David. "Poverty and Disrepute." In *Contemporary Social Problems,* ed. Robert K. Merton and Robert A. Nisbet. New York: Harcourt, Brace & World, 1966.

McDonald, Eugene T. *Understanding Those Feelings: A Guide for Parents of Handicapped Children.* Pittsburgh, Pa.: Stanwix House, 1962.

Meisgeier, Charles. *The Doubly Disadvantaged.* Austin, Tex.: University of Texas Press, 1966.

Mercer, Jane. *Labeling the Mentally Retarded.* Berkeley, Calif.: University of California Press, 1973.

Meyer, Agnes E. *Journey Through Chaos.* New York: Harcourt, Brace, 1943.

Meyerowitz, Joseph H. "Self Derogations in Young Retardates and Special Class Placement," *Child Development* 33 (1962): 443-451.

Montessori, Maria. *Spontaneous Activity in Education.* New York: Schocken, 1965.

Nader, Ralph, Peter Petkas, and Kate Blackwell. *Whistle Blowing.* New York: Bantam Books, 1972.

National Association for Retarded Children. Child Advocacy Project. Books I, II, III. New York: NARC, 420 Lexington Ave., N.Y., N.Y., 10017.

Noar, Gertrude. *Sensitizing Teachers to Ethnic Groups.* Anti-Defamation League of B'nai B'rith, distributed by Allyn & Bacon, New York.

O'Gorman, Ned. *The Wilderness and the Laurel Tree.* New York: Harper & Row, 1972.

Paulsen, Monrad G., "The Legal Rights of Children," *Childhood Education* (May 1974).

Perske, Robert, with illustrations by Martha Perske. *New Directions for Parents of Children Who are Retarded.* New York: Abingdon Press, 1973.

Pines, Maya. "Slum Children Must Make Up for Lost Time," *The New York Times Magazine* (October 15, 1967).

_____. *Revolution in Learning: The Years from Birth to Six.* New York: Har/Row Books, 1967.

Piven, Francis F., and Richard A. Cloward. *Regulating the Poor.* New York: Pantheon, 1971.

Platt, Anthony M. *The Child Savers: The Invention of Delinquency.* Chicago: University of Chicago Press, 1969.

_____ and Ruth Friedman. "The Limits of Advocacy: Occupational

Hazards in Juvenile Court," *Pennsylvania Law Review* 7 (1968): 1156-1184.

Practising Law Institute. *Legal Rights of the Mentally Handicapped.* New York: Practising Law Institute, 1133 Avenue of the Americas, N.Y., N.Y., 10036.

President's Committee on Mental Retardation. *The Six Hour Retarded Child.* Washington, D.C.: Department of Health, Education, and Welfare, Office of Education, 1969.

President's Task Force on the Mentally Handicapped. *Action Against Mental Disability.* Washington, D.C.: The Report of the President's Task Force, Supt. of Documents, 1970.

Raph, Jane Beasely. "The Language Development in Socially Disadvantaged Children," *Review of Educational Research* 35 (1965): 389-397.

Repo, Satu. *This Book is About Schools.* New York: Vintage, 1971.

The Rights of Children. Parts I and II. Cambridge, Mass.: Harvard Educational Review (November 1973 and February 1974), whole issues.

Riessman, Frank. *The Culturally Deprived Child.* New York: Harper & Row, 1962.

Ross, Donald. *A Public Citizen's Action Manual.* New York: Grossman Publishers, 1973.

Rowe, A.J.B. "Children's Hearings," *New Society* 19 (1972): 444-446.

Rubenstein, Annette T. *Schools Against Children, The Case for Community Control.* New York: Monthly Review Press, 1970.

Rubin, Sol. "Children as Victims of Institutionalization," *Child Welfare* 51 (1972).

Ryan, William. *Blaming the Victim.* New York: Vintage, 1972.

Schrag, Peter. *Village School Downtown.* Boston: Beacon Press, 1970.

_____ and Diane Divoky. *The Myth of the Hyperactive Child.* New York: Pantheon, 1975.

Schwebel, Milton. *Who Can Be Educated.* New York: Grove Press, 1968.

Siegel, E. *Special Education in the Regular Classroom.* New York: John Day, 1969.

Sigel, I.E. "How Intelligence Tests Limit Understanding of Intelligence," *Merrill-Palmer Quarterly of Behavior and Development* 9 (1963): 39-56.

Silberberg, N.E., and M.C. Silberberg. "The Bookless Curriculum: An Educational Alternative," *Journal of Learning Disabilities* 2 (1969): 302-307.

_____. "Is There Such a Thing as a Learning Disabled Child?" *Journal of Learning Disabilities* 4 (1971): 273-276.

_____. "Should Schools Have Psychologists?" *Journal of School Psychologists* 9 (1971): 321-328.

Silberman, Charles. *Crisis in the Classroom.* New York: Vintage, 1971.

Sloan, Irving J. *Youth and the Law.* Dobbs Ferry, N.Y.: Oceana, 1970.

Stephens, J.M.: *The Process of Schooling: A Psychological Examination.* New York: Holt, Rinehart & Winston, 1967.

Strouse, Jean. *Up Against the Law, The Legal Rights of People Under 21.* New York: Signet, 1970.

_____. "To Be Minor and Female," *Ms* (August 1972): 70.

Task Force on Children Out of School. *Suffer the Children, The Politics of Mental Health in Massachusetts.* Boston: The Task Force, 1972.

_____. *The Way We Go To School, The Exclusion of Children in Boston.* Boston: Beacon Press, 1971.

Trudeau, Elaine (editor). *Digest of State and Federal Laws: Education of Handicapped Children.* Reston, Va.: Council for Exceptional Children, 1972.

Van Stolk, Mary. "Who Owns The Child," *Childhood Education* (May 1974).

Walzer, Michael. *Political Action: A Practical Guide to Movement Politics.* New York: Quadrangle, 1971.

Warren, Roland L. *Studying Your Community.* New York: Free Press, 1955.

Wasserstein, Bruce, and Mark J. Green (editors). *With Justice For Some.* Boston: Beacon Press, 1970.

Webb, L. *Children with Special Needs in the Infants' School.* London: Colin Smythe, 1967.

Weinberg, Carl. *Education Is a Shuck.* New York: Morrow, 1974.

White House Conference on Children. *Report to the President.*

Washington, D.C.: U.S. Government Printing Office, 1971.

Wiggins, Kate. *Children's Rights.* Boston: Houghton and Mifflin, 1892.

Wise, Arthur E. *Rich Schools, Poor Schools.* Chicago: University of Chicago Press, 1972.

Wright, Beatrice. *Physical Disability-A Psychological Approach.* New York: Harper, 1960.

Wyatt, Susan. *The Mark: A Case for the Abolition of Grading.* Washington, D.C.: Center for Educational Reform, 2115 S Street, N.W.

Young, Don J. "Due Process and the Rights of Children," *Juvenile Court Judges Journal* 18 (1967): 102-105.

Young, L. *Wednesday's Children.* New York: McGraw Hill, 1964.

A List of Children's Rights Organizations

Action for Children's Television
46 Austin Street
Newtonville, Massachusetts
02160

Advance Foundation, Inc.
3502 S. Normandie Avenue
Los Angeles, California
90007

American Civil Liberties Union
85 Fifth Avenue
New York, New York
10011

American Friends Service Committee
112 S. 16th Street
Philadelphia, Pennsylvania
19102

Association of Volunteer Bureaus
of America
P.O. Box 7253
Kansas City, Missouri
64113

Center for Law and Social Policy
1600 20th Street, N.W.
Washington, D.C.
20009

Center for the Study of Student
Citizenship, Rights, and Responsibility
1145 Germantown Street
Dayton, Ohio
45408

Center on Human Policy
216 Ostrom Avenue
Syracuse, New York
13210

Child Welfare League of America
44 East 23rd Street
New York, N.Y. 10010

Children's Defense Fund
1763 R Street, N.W.
Washington, D.C.
20009

Children's Foundation
1026 17th Street, N.W.
Washington, D.C.
20036

Citizen's Committee for Children
112 East 19th Street
New York, New York
10003

Coordinating Council for Handicapped Children
407 S. Dearborn Street
Chicago, Illinois
60605

The Council for Exceptional Children
State-Federal Clearinghouse
1920 Association Drive
Reston, Virginia
22091

Crusade Against Hunger
National Council of Churches

475 Riverside Drive
New York, New York
10027

Day Care and Child Development
Council of America
1426 H Street, N.W., Suite 340
Washington, D.C.
20005

Education Exploration Center
3104 16th Avenue S.
Minneapolis, Minnesota
55407

ERIC/ECE (Educational Resources
Information Center, Early Child-
hood Education)
University of Illinois at Urbana-
Champaign
805 West Pennsylvania Avenue
Urbana, Illinois 61801

Freedom Through Equality, Inc.
152 West Wisconsin Avenue
Milwaukee, Wisconsin
53203

Health-Policy Advisory Committee
(PAC)
17 Murray Street
New York, New York
10007

International Association of
Parents of the Deaf
(IAPD)
Silver Spring, Maryland

Robert F. Kennedy Fellows Program
for the Rights of Children
1054 31st Street, N.W.
Washington, D.C.
20007

LEAP (A community action project)
540 East 13th Street
New York, New York

Life Center

Movement for a New Society
4722 Baltimore Avenue
Philadelphia, Pennsylvania 19143

Massachusetts Advocacy
2 Park Square
Boston, Massachusetts
02116

Mental Health Law Project
84 Fifth Avenue
New York, New York
10011
1751 N Street, N.W.
Washington, D.C.
20036

Mental Patients Liberation Project
P.O. Box 89
West Sommerville,
Massachusetts
02114

National Center for Child Advocacy
Department of HEW, Office of the
Secretary
P.O. Box 1182
Washington, D.C.
20013
A list of advocacy centers
throughout the country may be
obtained through this address.

National Center for Law and the
Handicapped
1235 N. Eddy Street
South Bend, Indiana
46617

National Center for Volunteer
Action
1735 I Street, N.W.
Washington, D.C. 20006

National Clearinghouse for Legal
Services
Northwestern University Law
School
710 N. Lake Shore Drive
Chicago, Illinois
60611

National Committee for Children
and Youth
  1145 19th Street, N.W.
  Washington, D.C.
  20036

National Council on the Rights of
the Mentally Impaired
  1600 20th Street, N.W.
  Washington, D.C.
  20009

National Juvenile Law Center
St. Louis University School of
Law
  3642 Lindell Boulevard
  St. Louis, Missouri
  63108

National Legal Aide and Defender
Association
  National Law Office
  1601 Connecticut Avenue, N.W.
  Washington, D.C.
  20009

National Welfare Rights Organization
  1419 H Street, N.W.
  Washington, D.C.
  20005

New Nation Seed Fund
  P.O. Box 4026
  Philadelphia, Pennsylvania
  19118
Funding agency for new schools,
concerned primarily with low-
income students.

The Office of Mental Retardation
Coordination
  Department of HEW
  Washington, D.C.
  20201

Organizer's Book Center
  P.O. Box 21066
  Washington, D.C.
  20009

The President's Committee on
Mental Retardation
  Seventh and D Streets, S.W.
  Washington, D.C.
  20201

Social Advocates for Youth
  315 Montgomery Street,
  Suite 1014
  San Francisco, California
  94104

Summerhill Collective
  137A West 14th Street
  New York, New York
  10011

Superintendent of Documents
  Government Printing Office
  Washington, D.C.

The Teacher's Store
  260 Park Avenue S. at 21st
Street
  New York, New York
  10010

Work Force
  Vocations for Social Change
  P.O. Box 13
  Canyon, California
  94516
  4911 Telegraph Avenue
  Box C
  Oakland, California
  94609

Youth Organizations United
  912 6th Street, N.W.
  Washington, D.C.
  20001

184

Index

Composed in Palatino by The New Republic Book
Company, Inc.

Printed and bound by The Maple Press Company,
York,Pennsylvania.

Designed by Gerard Valerio.